Collective Wisdom

The Power of Networking

Compiled by
Amb. Dr. Joan E. Wakeland (h.c.)

I0092908

No part of this publication may be reproduced, stored in a retrieval system, or transmitted in any form or by any means: electronic, mechanical, photocopying, recording or otherwise without the written permission of the publisher.

HAVANA BOOK GROUP LLC
43537 RIDGE PARK DRIVE
TEMECULA CA 92590

COPYRIGHT 2024 All rights reserved

ISBN: 979-8-9862647-8-3

Chapter Overview

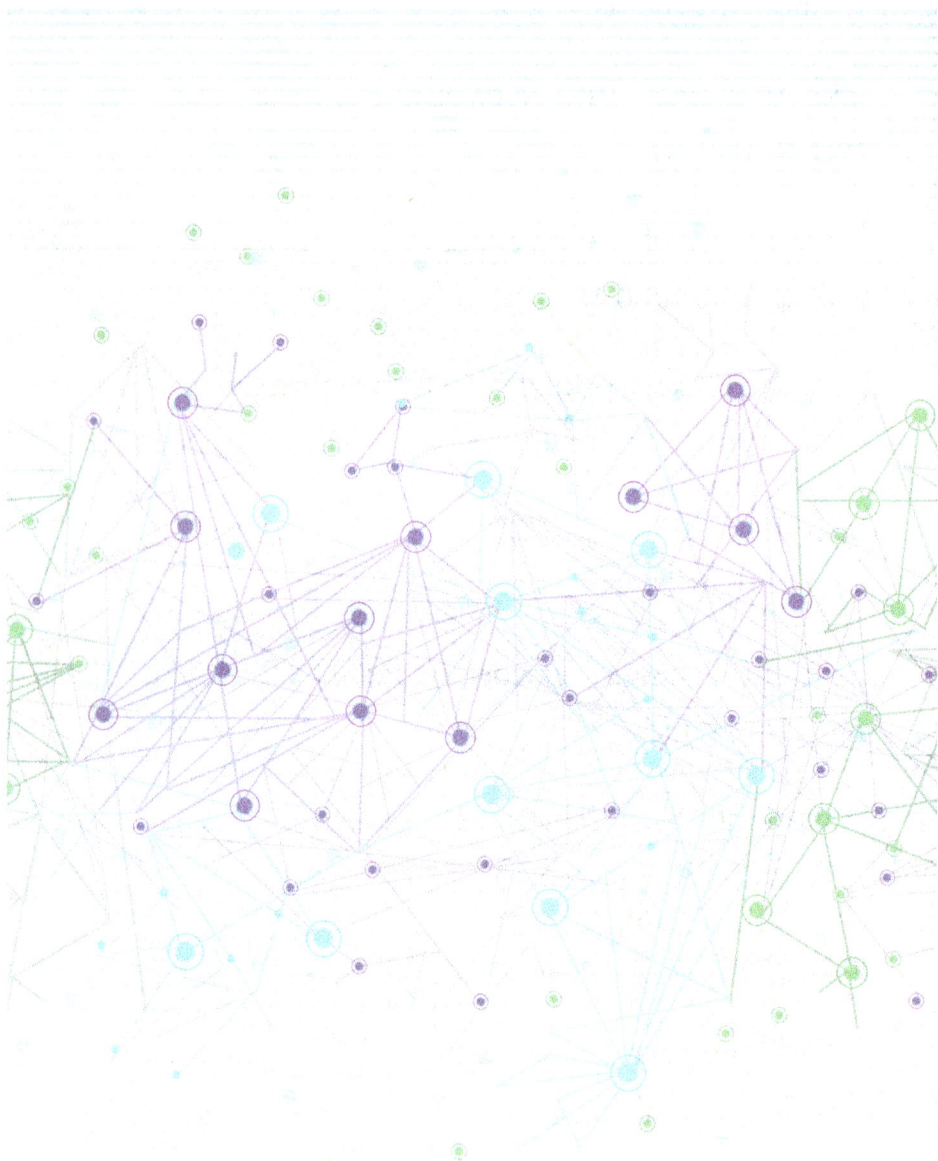

Dr. Caroline Makaka

Foreword

Amb. Dr. Joan E. Wakeland is one of the hardest working, passionate, inspiring , extraordinary, resilient, and dedicated woman who has transformed her life from darkness into light. She is a US International Speaker, a Best-Selling international author, a US No.1 author, and creator of products that have positive words of encouragement and kindness. On top of that she serves as the proud director of the GSFE Riverside, CA network and has received numerous awards for her work in the community including being honored as Citizen of the month, Call to Service awards from two Presidents, and numerous other awards from many dignitaries.

In a nutshell l describe her as the epitome of selfless love, a pillar of strength, and a go to companion.

This book highlights the importance of networking.

Network groups are groups of people who talk and share ideas, information, and resources and in the process, create great business connections.

Sometimes walking into a room full of strangers can bring nervousness. Networking usually involves meeting new people who share a profession, industry, or interests, and more importantly it helps to build professional relationships. Networking opens doors to new opportunities and facilitates the exchange of ideas and best practices.

Building connections with the right people at the right time is the vital key to networking which can help to take your career to the next stage . Networking is the process of making connections and building sustainable relationships. Networking clearly broadens one's horizons by giving a different perspective, another angle to view situations. It brings about fresh ideas that may have eluded you and essentially even brand-new information you were not aware of.

The confidence that can be brought by networking is immeasurable. It comes in leaps and bounds. Business Wise, networking is very much capable of increasing visibility and creating brand awareness. It promotes and exposes your brand to others whilst you gain knowledge about other brands, too. Networking also improves enhanced learning and development. Needless to say, there will be an increase in referrals.

Being associated with certain people in your network leads to greater exposure. Here's how this works. If you're doing

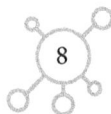

networking right, you'll have instances or opportunities to associate with well-known figures in your industry. That could be through engagement on social platforms, collaborations, and maybe even direct endorsements.

In Conclusion, to build the most sustainable network, have a networking plan and create your Goals and your purpose. Set goals to add to your contacts; follow up immediately. Get to know your contacts. Stay connected. Ask questions. Invest time and effort to help others. Nurture your own network, facilitate the meeting of contacts, and invite new people to join.

Professor Caroline Makaka is a woman of many talents and an expert in many industries---a lady with a vision and a mission to shape the future of the world through courage, strength, resilience, hope, tenacity, and transformational power to create a better world. She is the Founder/President/CEO of LOANI - Ladies of All Nations International - and Creator of We Are the Change World Movement. Her areas of expertise encompass a wide range of skills such as Philanthropy, Global Leadership, Global Cultural Exchange, Education, Non-profit Leadership, Charities, International Project Management, Human Resources, Leadership, Individual Counseling, Equality and Diversity, Youth Empowerment, and Recognition Awards.

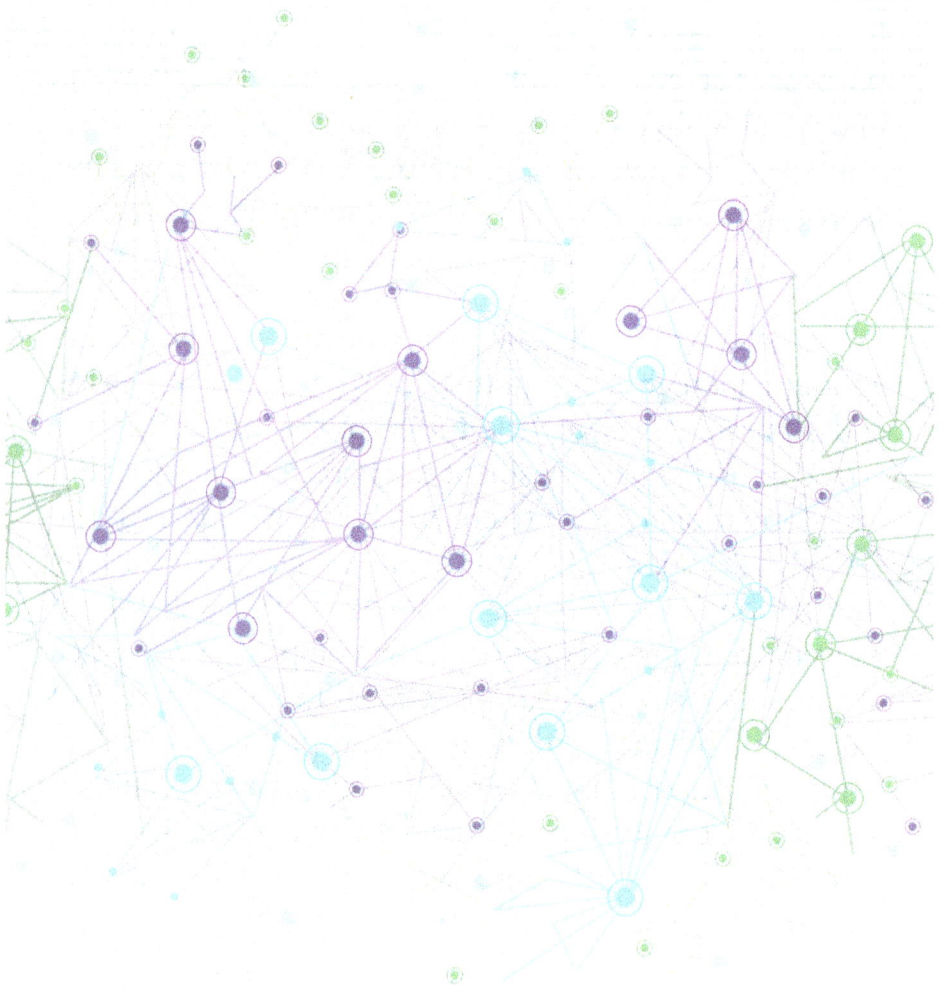

Dr. Angeline Benjamin (h.c.)

Put Networking As One Of Your Top Priorities

First, we need to ask ourselves why having a priority is important if we want to achieve our goals. Prioritization is important because it allows us to give attention to the tasks that are urgent and important so that later, we can focus on the lower-priority tasks. Once we are clear that having priorities is important, then we are able to make better and quicker decisions that guide our life choices.

For you to resonate with my message, I will share how I was able to achieve my goal by creating a priority list. One of my goals in 2020 was to write a book, and I wanted to complete it in six months. Keep in mind I had never written a book before. I wrote articles, reports, etc. But writing a book was completely beyond my imagination. With the help of my mentor, who empowered and inspired me, I created a plan and activities that related to completing my book. This became my business priority in 2020.

I understood that we couldn't have too many priorities because I knew if we had too many, we would be overwhelmed. Keep in mind that priorities can change once we achieve a specific goal. Before I get into the how-to set priorities, I want to share a few examples of priorities that you can relate to. Here are the examples:

- Health
- Family
- Relationship
- Personal growth
- Business
- Money
- Volunteering

You may have your own priority list based on what you want to achieve in a certain period of time.

Setting a priority list for you is unique to you. You need to have a clear vision of what you want to achieve for the next 12 months. You need to be able to visualize and define it.

One thing I realized was just having one goal to finish my book is not realistic. I needed to have a balanced life. So, I created a life priority for 2020 in late December 2019. Below are my priorities for 2020.

1. Health/Wellness: if I am not healthy, I will not be able to accomplish my goal for 2020.

2. Business: if I don't have business as one of my priorities, I will not be able to finish my book in 6 months.

3. Relationship – I need healthy relationships with my husband, close family, and friends as a support system to create balance in my life.

Because the topic of this chapter is networking as one of our priorities, I am going to focus on Business.

As an example, I will share with you my Business Priorities. (#2)

You need to choose the method that works for you. Finding the right prioritization technique is personal. I suggest using the method that makes sense and works for you.

I used the ABC method because it is simple and makes sense to me.

Box A: Urgent tasks

Box B: Important tasks

Box C: Anything else after I completed Box A and B tasks.

Since writing a book was new to me, and writing is not my strong skill, I decided to hire a coach to help me accomplish this goal. First, I searched for a coach with whom I could relate (I put that task in Box A – Urgent). I chose a coach who understood what I needed to accomplish. I hired her and signed a contract, and we created a schedule. One of my Urgent Tasks was completed!

We were going to meet on a weekly basis until the first phase was completed, and then we would work on the next schedule. We planned to start on April 20, 2020. What we did not expect was that the COVID-19 pandemic hit the US in early March. So instead of having a live meeting, we decided to have a virtual meeting using Zoom. We had to adjust and not postpone the plan. I created my plan for what I needed to do daily, weekly. I achieved my goal and launched my book on November 17, 2020.

Here are examples of what I had to do daily as a priority using the ABC method.

Box A: This includes anything critical and urgent that I must complete on that day. If I do not complete these tasks, there will be serious consequences. Example: I must complete one thing I assigned on that day related to writing my book.

Box B: These are important tasks. I can only complete the tasks in Box B after I complete the task in Box A. Example: Attend the virtual session with my coach, review what I have completed, learn new things, and plan on what I have to complete for next week. Why did I put this task on Box B instead of Box A? If my coach has to reschedule for the next day, there will not be a serious consequence. I can still complete my urgent tasks.

Box C: These tasks are not urgent and important;

there is no consequence if I do not do the tasks on that day. Example: Reply to emails that are not urgent or important.

Keep in mind when I put the tasks in Box A, I must be realistic and have the discipline to complete the tasks before I go to Box B. Therefore, I could not put too many tasks that were urgent/critical on that day. I have to be realistic about the time to complete the tasks in Box A. The same thing happened in Box B; I had to make sure I did not put too many things that were important to complete on that day since I may not be able to complete them. Therefore, time management is very important in prioritizing our tasks.

Since the topic of this chapter is about putting "Networking as one of our top priorities," I will lay out this plan using my ABC Plan as an example. If it makes more sense for you to use the other methods, please do so.

By now, after reading the previous chapter in this book, you understand the power of networking in building your business. I am providing a tool that you need to have in your task related to "networking" which should be one of your top priorities on a daily basis.

Here are the examples:

Day 1 of the week:

Box A – attend networking meetings you find a good fit for your business. Depending upon what other tasks you decided to put in this box, you must attend at least one networking meeting.

In Box B – attend the second or third networking meetings, but you must attend the one you put in Box A first.

In Box C: you may schedule other events after you complete the tasks in Box A and B – This should be non-negotiable.

Day 2, 3, 4, and 5 of the weeks – follow the same concept as I gave you on Day 1.

To make this task easy to manage, you need to add all your urgent and important tasks/schedules to your calendar. I use Google Calendar. It works very well for me. I sync my calendar to my computer, cell phone, tablet, etc. Because I associate with color better, I used colors to identify the task categories. After all urgent and important tasks are entered into my calendar, then I enter Box C tasks in the time slot I have left. I do not fill my calendar with all business tasks with no space to take a break or do my personal urgent/important tasks.

In summary, here are my life experience tips:

Tip # 1:

Since networking meetings are one of the important events as our urgent task, add in your calendar all the recurring networking events you set as urgent tasks to attend for the whole year (or whatever timeline you have to achieve this goal). Be disciplined not to delete this urgent networking meeting if you want to attend networking meetings as one of your top priorities. Follow-up calls/emails, etc., are important tasks that you need to add following each networking meeting.

Tip # 2:

Do not feel guilty about adding the time/schedule to your calendar for your urgent and important personal tasks. My examples: breaks, workouts, walking my dogs, preparing meals for my husband, medical appointments, etc.

Tip #3:

Put in your calendar the starting time for your business day and end of business day. This will help you schedule your appointment effectively.

Tip #4:

Crises happen! Disasters happen! Illnesses happen! Unexpected events happen! How do we manage these? We have to learn to adjust. Do your best and move on!

These valuable tools and tips will definitely prioritize your business networking-related tasks as your top priorities, which are your urgent tasks. Execute and add these tasks to your schedule now! Do the things you can control and let go of the things you can't control. Strive for excellence!

QUESTIONS FOR CONSIDERATION:

Do I need an accountability partner?

What is the best way to manage my time?

Do I use a system to track my appointments?

I have too many priorities in a day, how can I manage emails and Facebook?

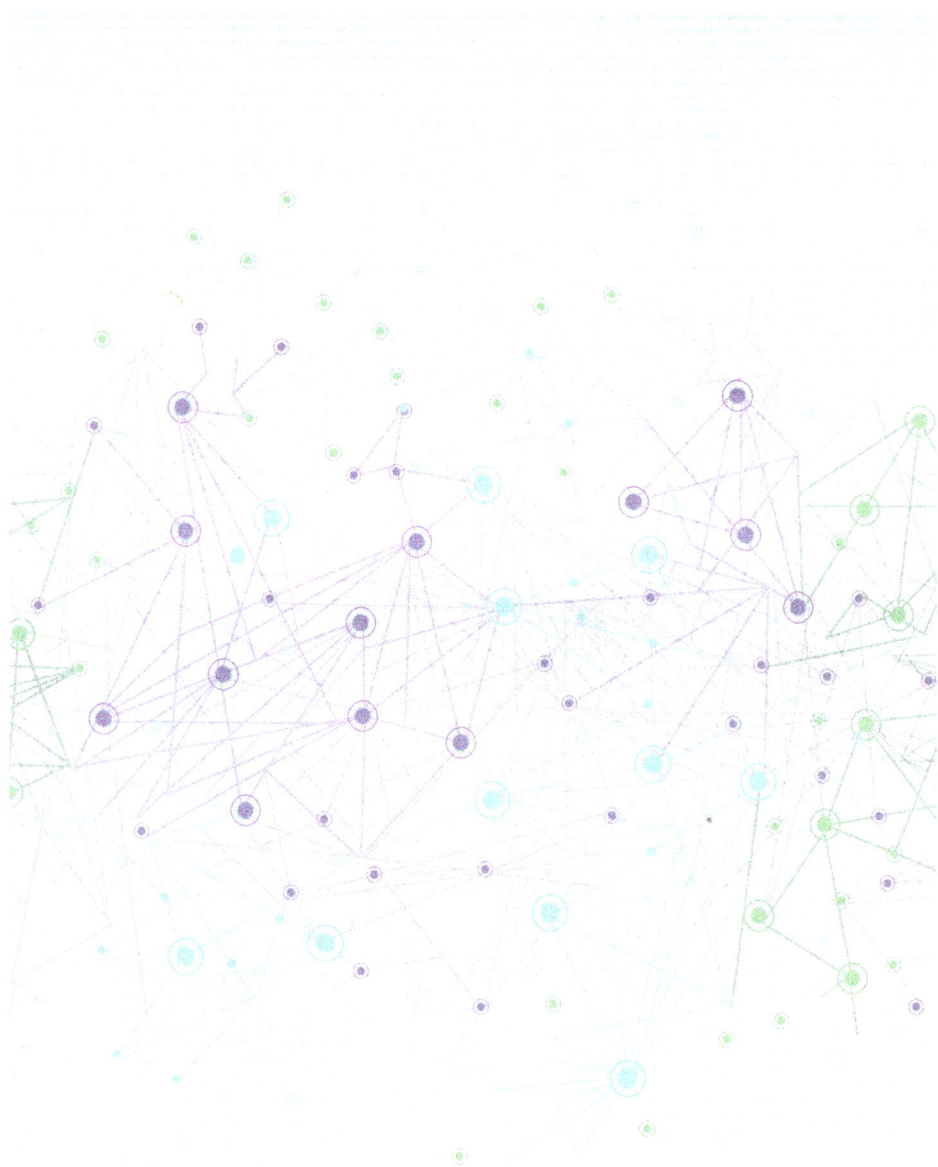

Dr. AnGele Cade (h.c.)

The Journey To Entrepreneurship

To the budding entrepreneur, take a moment and envision your dream, your prize, your future. This is not simply a fleeting idea or an abstract concept, but your driving force, your purpose. To succeed in this constantly evolving world, we must learn to firmly hold our vision, remaining steady amidst the whirlwind of distractions. And an integral part of this journey is the art of networking.

When we speak of networking, it's not just about transactional interactions or the gathering of contacts. Rather, it is about the cultivation of relationships, genuine exchanges that invite growth, mutual understanding, and collective advancement.

As we journey through the entrepreneurial landscape, the pull of countless distractions threatens to derail us from our path. Yet, it is our sacred duty to remain steadfast.

Hold your vision steadily, that is your guiding light.

Every entrepreneur must understand their path, recognizing the value of each connection in their grand entrepreneurial voyage. Every interaction, every relationship contributes a unique thread to your tapestry of success.

The world around us is a symphony of ideas. Let us tune in to this beautiful music, opening our minds and hearts to the diverse insights that come our way. Often, the most profound wisdom is hidden in the most unexpected conversations. Keep your mind receptive and your heart open.

The cornerstone of networking is authenticity. Seek to foster connections in a spirit of honesty, respect, and mutual growth. Our world craves genuineness, and in an environment of trust and transparency, the seeds of true growth can flourish.

We are living in an era of technological wonders. Platforms like LinkedIn, Twitter, and Instagram are not mere tools, but powerful bridges connecting us to like-minded individuals across the globe. Utilize these platforms to extend your reach, share your journey, and build meaningful relationships.

Networking is a dance of reciprocity. As you reach out for help, be equally willing to offer your support. Share your wisdom freely, offer assistance when you can. It is in the sharing of knowledge and resources that we strengthen our bonds and transform our relationships.

Patience is an essential virtue in networking. The fruits of genuine relationships take time to ripen. Keep your focus firmly on your vision, while patiently nurturing your present relationships.

The journey to entrepreneurship is akin to navigating a stormy sea. It is fraught with challenges and obstacles, demanding courage, and resilience. In these times, remember that you are not alone. Your network of relationships stand with you, a beacon of strength and support.

Networking is more than just a strategy, it is a journey of self-discovery, learning, and growth. It allows us to learn from others, inspire change, and make a lasting impact. It's not only the destination that matters, but the rich tapestry of experiences that makes the journey truly rewarding.

So, my fellow entrepreneurs, hold your vision steadfastly. Embrace focus, patience, and authenticity. Your network is a fertile ground teeming with opportunities. Even when one door closes, countless others stand ready to open.

Continue forging ahead. Your vision, your prize, is well within your reach. The world is waiting for the unique gifts you have to offer. So, shine your light brightly, build connections with care, and create the future you've always envisioned. This journey, with all its challenges and triumphs, is yours to embark upon, and every step brings you closer to your prize. So go forth, hold your vision steadfastly, and let the power of networking guide your path to success.

As you venture on, remember to cultivate a mindset of gratitude. Appreciate the people who form your network, each bringing a unique perspective and value. In every interaction, be it a casual conversation or a formal meeting, there is always a lesson to be learned. Every relationship you nurture is a chance to expand your horizons and enrich your understanding of the world.

Embrace humility. As you seek to expand your network, understand that everyone you meet has something to teach you. Even the most seasoned entrepreneurs can learn from the most unexpected sources. Recognize and value the wisdom in others, for it's the diversity of thoughts that fuels innovation and growth.

In the context of networking, communication is key. Speak clearly, listen attentively, and remember that sometimes, the most impactful conversations are those where you listen more than you speak. Learning to listen is an art, one that yields insight and fosters mutual understanding.

Invest time and effort into your relationships. Networking is not an overnight process, and relationships need nurturing to grow. Check in with your contacts, show genuine interest in their endeavors, and provide support when possible. It's through these consistent efforts that you strengthen your relationships and build a robust network.

Be persistent. The road to successful networking may be long and arduous, but the benefits are immense. If a connection doesn't yield immediate results, don't be discouraged. Remember, it's about building a relationship, not a transaction.

Let the essence of networking infuse all aspects of your entrepreneurial journey. The skills and attitudes you develop in networking - empathy, patience, openness, and resilience - are not confined to this aspect alone. They contribute to your personal growth, improving your ability to connect with people in all areas of your life.

To close, remember that the entrepreneurial journey is unique for each individual, and there's no one-size-fits-all approach to success. Stay true to your values, keep your vision clear, and let your passion fuel your journey.

Your vision is your prize, the shining beacon that guides your path. Keep your gaze fixed on it. Despite the turbulence that may come your way, remember that you are never alone. Your network, each connection you've nurtured, is with you. They are your allies, your guides, and your support.

So, continue your journey, fellow entrepreneur. Hold your vision steadfastly. Keep your eye on the prize. The world awaits your unique gifts. Shine your light brightly, build your connections wisely, and harness the power of networking to create the future you envision. The path is yours to tread, each step bringing you closer to your prize. Embrace the journey with all its twists and turns, for it is in this journey that you'll find the true essence of success.

As you traverse this entrepreneurial journey, equip yourself with self-belief. The faith in your ability to overcome hurdles and find a way where there seems to be none. This self-belief acts as your inner compass, always guiding you towards your vision.

Always remember that networking is an exercise in personal growth as much as it is professional. The process of connecting, sharing, and growing together extends beyond the realm of entrepreneurship. It permeates your whole being, making you more open, receptive, and empathetic.

Remember to treat each relationship you nurture with respect and sincerity. Your network reflects your values, your vision, and your passion. To have people in your life who support your vision and add value to your journey is a treasure of immeasurable worth.

In the process of networking, aim not just to learn but also to inspire. Share your story, your struggles, and triumphs. You never know how your journey may inspire someone else, just as others have inspired you. In this sharing, there's a mutual growth that's highly rewarding.

Stay adaptable. Our world is dynamic, constantly evolving. To succeed, you need to be flexible, adjusting your approach to align with changing circumstances, yet never losing sight of your vision. Flexibility aids in not just surviving but thriving amidst the unpredictability of the entrepreneurial journey.

To the budding entrepreneur, networking may seem daunting, yet remember, everyone you meet is on a journey of their own. They have their challenges, their triumphs, their dreams. Approach each interaction with an open mind and heart. Celebrate the diversity of experiences and thoughts, for this is the soil where great ideas and partnerships grow.

In closing, let me remind you that networking is not a destination, but an ongoing journey. It is the path that leads you to your vision, your prize. Every conversation, every relationship, every shared insight brings you one step closer to it.

As you continue on this path, hold your vision steadfastly. Be patient, be persistent, and most importantly, be true to yourself. The entrepreneurial journey is filled with challenges, but with focus and a strong network, you are well-equipped to navigate this path.

So go forth, fellow entrepreneur. Continue nurturing your relationships, building your network, and paving the path to your envisioned future. Stay committed to your journey, hold your vision steadfastly, and always remember - your eye is on the prize. The world needs your unique contributions, and every step you take is a testament to your courage, resilience, and unwavering focus. Keep moving forward, for your prize is well within your grasp.

QUESTIONS FOR CONSIDERATION:

Networking is not just transactional. Why?

What are my core values?

What can I offer to grow other people's business?

Am I open to collaboration?

Am I willing to listen and learn from unexpected sources?

How much time/money am I willing to invest in improving myself and others?

Virginia Clarke

Growth – Personally And In Business

It is with humble gratitude and boundless appreciation I begin this chapter with a resounding shoutout to my Mother Darlene. Without her, I would have never found the love of the written word, nor the confidence to share my story with the world. Her love forever fuels the fire that dances within me. Thanks, Mom.

According to Funk & Wagnalls Standard Desk Dictionary, growth is "the act or process of growing." So, what does growth, or the act or process of growing look like for me personally and in my business?

The end of 2019 and the beginning of 2020 were a game-changer for me. I had just found out I was losing my job of 10 years, due to government cuts, and I was spiraling out of control. I was drinking more than I had in years and finally hit rock bottom. January 27, 2020, was a day I'll never forget. I realized I had to quit drinking, or I would lose everything I worked so hard for. This decision was the first step on my journey of personal growth.

Sobriety brought with it a newfound ability to face challenges head-on and find healthier ways to cope with difficulties. It was a process of learning new coping mechanisms, making better decisions, and rediscovering myself without the influence of alcohol. I learned how to get along with myself. It involved navigating through ups and downs, exploring different aspects of myself, and embracing new experiences and perspectives. It's a continuous journey, and every step I take toward understanding myself better contributes to my overall growth and well-being. What a wild ride this has been!

Fast forward to 2023, when I was first approached to write a chapter on networking, I absolutely was not going to say yes! I am not a writer I thought, those dark clouds of self-doubt and fear slowly creeping back in, after I had worked so hard to keep them out. I decided to make fear my friend, so when it was my turn to be asked, I surprised myself and ended up saying "I'm in", (that was huge personal growth for me right there) and then the panic and chaos set in! How on earth was I going to do this? Writing is absolutely not my talent! I cannot do this! And worst of all I wasn't even sure of where to start, I'd never written something on this scale before. So, I sat down and started jotting down notes about my personal and professional growth over the years. Realizing I did have something to say eased the doubts that plagued my mind and as I stared at the blank page, I started to write.

I concluded that I didn't need to be a born writer to share my knowledge and experiences. What mattered was my passion for the subject matter and my genuine desire to help others through my words. I embraced the concept of baby steps, acknowledging the many small but significant strides I had taken throughout my journey. I decided to share myself.

Overcoming the challenges and hardships I've faced, such as the absence of love and affection from my alcoholic father, and recognizing the unhealthy coping mechanisms I developed, like using alcohol to numb the pain I was dealing with, are significant milestones in my life.

Acknowledging that alcohol was not a solution and that the problems always found a way of resurfacing showed my growing self-awareness. It took strength and courage to confront my pain and face it head-on. By doing so, I had taken a powerful step toward my healing and personal transformation. Becoming the strong, amazing woman I am today, one who believes in her abilities and knows she can achieve anything she sets her mind to, is a testament to my resilience and determination. It's important to recognize and celebrate progress. We must remember our personal growth is a reflection of our inner strength and the work we've put into our self improvement journey.

As I write this, I have now celebrated over 1200 days of sobriety. That was and still is enormous personal growth for me. Yeah me! I cherish each day, and I am becoming a more mindful being. This journey of personal growth has led me to become a more understanding mother and positive role model for my teenage son showing my commitment to nurturing and supporting his development, and my increased compassion, as a wife to my husband of 22 years demonstrates my dedication to maintaining a healthy and loving relationship. By embarking on this journey of personal growth, I have not only enhanced my own well-being but also positively influenced the lives of my loved ones. We must remember to celebrate our progress and continue embracing opportunities for self-improvement and self-discovery.

During this journey of self-discovery, I met an accomplished mentor who quickly became a friend, Dr. Laurie Davis, who introduced me to the wonderful world of self-worth, something I didn't even realize I was lacking in my life. Taking back my self-worth was indeed an enlightening growth process. It involved acknowledging my strengths, embracing my flaws, (and boy do I have flaws!), It also involved learning to love and accept myself unconditionally. Remember, by cultivating our self-worth, we empower ourselves to set healthy boundaries, pursue our passions, and make choices that align with our values. I was able to find peace within myself and strengthen my relationship with my father before his passing in 2022.

Expressing my thoughts and feelings to him while he was alive brought me a sense of closure and allowed me to let go of any lingering shame or guilt. Forgiveness was a transformative process for both of us, by forgiving my father and myself, I experienced a profound sense of liberation and emotional growth. It was a true testament to my resilience, inner strength, and self-worth that I was able to release the burdens of the past and move forward with a clear heart and soul.

Meeting Laurie also led me down a different path to becoming an Empowerment facilitator with her organization, Self Worth the Missing Link. This brings in my professional side of growth and networking. I sat on the fence before I took the leap to start my business. What would my family think? Could I, do it? Was I going to be successful? That self-doubt has a way of sneaking back in at the most inopportune times. I took the leap!

For my business, networking has helped me establish new partnerships that have allowed me to share my vast knowledge, exchange ideas, and collaborate on new projects, along the lines of this one. It has broadened my horizons. Networking is indeed a valuable tool for any business owner. By establishing new partnerships, we open doors to opportunities for growth and expansion. Through networking, we can meet like-minded individuals, potential clients, and collaborators who can contribute to our success. By actively engaging in networking, I was investing in my business's growth and building a strong professional support system. Remember, networking is a continuous process, so it's important to nurture these connections over time.

What does personal and professional growth have to do with a book about networking you may ask, I wondered that myself when I started, but when I looked back on how far I had come as an individual and in my professional life, I realized that networking was an essential component for both my personal and professional growth, by having that strong support network we can accomplish anything we set our minds to, and without that support network, I would not have grown into the woman I am today. I would not have had the courage to start my own business, and I would never have met the wonderfully supportive organization I have been blessed to be part of.

Networking helped both my personal and professional life by expanding my social circle where I was allowed to meet and learn from others with a vast diversity of backgrounds, ages, religions, and experiences. It gave me the courage to step out of my comfort zone and say yes to things I never would have said yes to. Like writing this chapter for one. I choose to ignore my limitations. Looking back, I realized that saying "I'm in" had been a pivotal moment in my personal growth. It pushed me beyond my comfort zone, allowing me to discover hidden strengths and capabilities. This journey has been filled with self-discovery, learning, and growth—one baby step at a time.

Remember that personal growth is an ongoing process, and there will be ups and downs along the way. But as long as we continue to believe in ourselves and stay committed to our personal development, we have the power to create a fulfilling and meaningful life for ourselves. We need to keep nurturing our inner strength, seeking new challenges, and embracing opportunities for growth. We have come a long way, and there is so much more ahead for us to achieve.

QUESTIONS FOR CONSIDERATION:

What new experiences am I embracing?

Am I loving myself first?

Am I standing in my own way and self-sabotage my purpose?

Is fear holding me back?

What is my passion, how can I share my expertise!

On a scale from 1 through 10, where is my self-worth?

How can I improve my personal growth?

How can I build a community of supporters through networking?

Dr. Laurie Davis (h.c.)

The Envelope

"The stranger standing beside us, with the proper connection could be our next very best friend ever." Dr Laurie Davis

The year was 1994 and I was about to embark on one of the most amazing journeys of my business career. I was at my desk and more bills but amongst them was a larger envelope with a beautiful logo and design. I opened it carefully as my curiosity was up as to whom would be sending me such a package.

An organization was offering six days of intense training to move a person from where one might be now and to share the art of facilitation and why anyone who was in the workshop/training and educational fields should learn how to become an effective facilitator. I was deeply intrigued and remember reading every word. I could feel the excitement mounting as I was so impressed with the offering until I got to the bottom line. The investment was 15000.00 US!

I did not have 1500.00 let alone 15000.00. I talked with my husband Ron who was my business partner as well and he said, Laurie if this were something that would benefit our business then we will find a way to make it happen. Sure, enough after selling some items and getting a loan from a friend who believed in me the registration went in.

The location was Toronto and that would mean plane tickets or drive there. Deciding to drive we planned to venture up on our beautiful burgundy Honda Goldwing and make a holiday of it. We decided to stay with friends in Toronto which saved us lots of money. We were busy putting the necessary people together who could help make this happen.

Once the details were in place, we were off on a ride that was about to change the course of our lives forever. The trip was uneventful, and it took us 3 days to get to our destination. I left a business card in every public washroom I visited!

I was happy to meet all my co classmates as there were ten of us from all over North America. The training was very intense, and it was here I realized I was not nearly as confident as I thought I was. We were grilled and stripped down so we could be rebuilt and refurbished just like an old car. I fear that I was a handful. I operated having lots of negative programming in place and being forced to shift the beliefs that were no longer supporting was challenging.

In my group was a man named Tom from Seattle Washington. He and I enjoyed many conversations together. On the last day of class Tom invited us to get on our bike and come to Seattle for a couple of weeks. We were invited to stay with him and his family. Having exhausted most of our funds we either had to head home in one direction or pursue an adventure to the west. We chose the west.

Tom was fifth generation Mormon, and we had no idea the amount of networking that was about to take place. Tom was also a very sought-after Real Estate Appraiser and the best entrepreneur I had met to date in the world of small home-based businesses. This was 1994 and guess who had a computer. Yes, Tom certainly was a forward thinker.

After two weeks of sharing, talking, meeting new people, Tom and I decided to use the training we had received to create a product. This project deemed it necessary that we extend our stay. We would be there for the next year!

My role was to create the product, network, and market it so we could then have Tom be our salesperson. I was so happy to have met Tom, which now leads me to my next big surprise. I was anxious to get out there and meet people. The city of Seattle opened its arms to me with just the meeting of one beautiful woman named Jean.

I attended a Women's Breakfast Networking group. I knew not one person in the room. I sat at a table where there was an empty chair. It was quite a chance meeting but there are no accidents. Jean was on my right petite pretty woman in her sixties at the time. I asked her what she did for a business and her response came back in such a way as I have never heard of before that day.

Jeans response to me was "What do you need, as that will be my next assignment." I was blown away. She informed me she built a business by just asking that one question and then she would go to work. I explained that I was new in town. I am a Canadian who has a project that I was not to get out there and I need to meet people.

She responded she could help me with that and invited me to the Seattle Rotary Club for lunch the next day as her guest. There would be 700 people there and would that help me out to go and meet some folks. I could not believe it. I had a connection with the Rotary Club back east where maybe 20 people met for lunch. My friend the late Helen Bourne and I were the first two females to join the club back in the day when women were finally accepted into those male circles. Now lunch with 700 terrific!

The following day I met Jean and she shared that at each luncheon they have feature tables at the front where special interest groups would eat together. On this day, the feature table was for anyone who has ridden on a motorcycle or who owns one. Was this by design? I was beginning to feel that way for sure.

Jean took me to the feature table, introduced me and I sat with that group while Jean networked some more. When I told the guys that we had travelled a total of six thousand miles one way on our bike they just wanted to know more and more about me and what I was doing there. That day changed everything again.

The bonus to networking with the men at that feature table also got me some press. The city newspaper always reported the events and timetables of the Rotary Club so lo and behold the next day our feature table was plastered on the front page and a story of how a visiting Rotarian had travelled six thousand miles and was attending their luncheon. As a point of interest this at the time was the largest Rotary Club on the planet and here, I was amid it.

My heart sang as I thought of the kindness afforded to me by my beautiful new friend Jean. I wanted to thank her, so I invited her to join me the next day at our apartment for lunch. I made some egg salad sandwiches and a cup of tea which I thought would be nice. Keeping things simple has always worked for me. I was somewhat embarrassed by our meagerness at the time but that was my best for that day. Jean was more than happy to drop by.

The buzzer rang out and there she was at my front door. Please go back and read my opening quote as this has been my experience. She threw off her expensive Italian leather pumps, plopped herself down on my sofa and put her feet up on the cushions. She expressed how she felt she had just died and gone to heaven. I was not sure what she meant.

In the next hour as we were sipping tea and having our sandwich, she shared who she was and her story. She had spent her life married to a high-profile politician who had gone down during Watergate and left her on the doorstep with five little kids to raise. Being an at home Mom she had no skills or training. All she knew was that she loved helping others to move forward particularly in business. She packed up the kids and moved to Seattle. She started her consulting firm and attracted a new and loving husband.

At this point I am thinking, a cup of tea and an egg salad sandwich. Yikes! I started apologizing for the simplicity of our lunch and she informed me she longs for those times when one does not have to put on airs but get a chance to just be oneself and relax.

Jean would be the source of my meeting the most incredible people. That year in Seattle became the foundation of my business. My first product entitled The Road to High Places found its place in many hands worldwide for the next three decades.

This all happened because of opening one envelope and saying yes.

QUESTIONS FOR CONSIDERATION:

I am excited about self-development; however, I don't have the money.

Thinking outside the box what are some ways I could get funding?

What belief systems do I have that no longer serves me?

Do I have to see many people in a networking event to think if my attendance was worth it?

Think about a time when you only met one influencer who could impact your business, and you wanted to build a relationship. What happened? Were you successful in getting that person's attention?

Sherrill Franklin

Selective Networking or This Not That

What does it take to build a successful business?

The title of this chapter is "Selective Networking," but it is important to realize that selectivity (is that a word? Well, if it was not before, it is now) does not first come into play at the networking stage which is far downstream in the business-building process. Selectivity governs the process of building a successful business from concept to multi-million-dollar status.

When the budding entrepreneur gets the "I want my own business" bug, the selection process starts. Often, at that stage, the selectivity is subconscious. The person has been mildly dissatisfied with the local coffee shop for years, wishing they offered better coffee and a more inviting atmosphere, or has just had it with the sixth housekeeping service that does a sloppy job, or has vaguely heard friends saying, "The bracelet you made for Ana is just beautiful. Can you make me one?" Suddenly the thoughts crystallize, "I can do that.," "I'd like to do that.," "Why couldn't I do that?"

Now the selections continue, "Keep my day job and start this on the side?" "Jump in the deep end and quit right away," "Use my savings, or take out a loan?" Every moment of every day after the initial realization, the budding entrepreneur must refine her choices, selecting this and not that, so the business begins to look more and more like "my" business, not the three or four similar businesses out in the marketplace.

All along the decisions continue to be made, until one day we have a business entity, sole proprietorship, partnership, LLC, ready to offer goods or services to the marketplace.

Now since this is a chapter in a book on networking, I suspect that several of my readers are not yet feeling engaged. Many of us, whether through inexperience, lack of funds, or simple caution, choose to enter the business-owner space by partnering with an established company, either through a franchise, or through a social marketing/network-marketing company. Not for us the selectivity of goods or service, location, funding, sole proprietorship, or LLC; we enter the space with what I like to call a business-in-a-box, one with an identity and a marketing plan already in place. In return for these benefits, we are agreeing to use our contacts and work ethics to help build the brand and increase market share for our company.

So, let us get engaged by focusing on the network marketing model, because what we say about this model can be easily extrapolated to the franchise or independent business entity models. Notice that the company that we are going to join already has its marketing plan in place. This means that the company has already identified the demographics – age range, income range, sex, cultural outlook, etc. of the people it wants to reach. Ideally, therefore, we should take a look at the company's mission and vision before we put our money down. Does it sound as though the company and distributor will be going in the same direction? And now let us keep it real. Most of us in the network marketing space did not do that! I certainly did not. A friend introduced me to the products, I totally fell in love with them, liked what she was doing, and the rest is history. But, reasoned research or impulsive leap, however we got here, we now have to build our business inside our company's business; we have to network.

Remember that marketing is not networking. Think of marketing as the one-way-street, and networking as the two-way street. In marketing, we identify the people we want to reach, craft the messages that we think will attract them and send them out. The people on the other end are passive recipients of our messages. In networking, both parties are active. We say hello, but it is not networking unless we are saying hello and leaving room for the other person to respond. The following statement, "Hi, I'm Sherill, 'Nature's Designs' custom jewelry. Let me give you, my card. The QR code on the back has my location and a coupon for 10% off your first purchase for anyone in our networking group. I hope you can come by soon.," is not networking, it is simply verbal marketing.

What is networking, anyway? We can think of it as a process of interacting with others in order to build rapport, exchange information and develop lasting connections. If we have joined a good company, our fellow distributors or consultants will immediately introduce us to networking groups where we can start that process of "interacting with others." This what I call "formal" organized networking. However, we meet people all day long. It is important to remember that contact, in an informal setting, between people with common interests, can still be networking. A single point of common interest can start an interaction which can lead to those lasting contacts.

At this point we have "selected" our way down from the idea of a business, to choosing the type of business, to identifying marketing versus networking. Now here we are, at the formal networking event put on monthly by the Chamber of Commerce. We are armed with boundless enthusiasm, a fancy digital business card and samples, getting ready to be selective about our networking.

Selective Networking is often understood to be encapsulated in this sentence, "Don't spend time trying to sell a BMW to someone with a Ford Focus budget." For those in other arenas, we could translate as, "Don't spend time trying to sell anti-aging skincare to an eighteen-year-old.," or "Quit trying to sell leather boots to a vegan." However, this only "Selective networking IF we are actually networking. Many salespeople and business owners engage in the following spoken and unspoken exchange. "Hi, I'm Clark with Raceway BMW." "Hi there, I'm Joe. I work for Jiffy Lube." (Clark now thinks, "Jiffy Lube. He can't afford a BMW." He drops the conversation and moves on.") He doesn't take the extra two minutes of conversation to discover that Joe is Joseph Warren, VP of Operations for the Western Region of the Jiffy Lube corporation and does happen to be in the market for high-end cars!

The foregoing example demonstrates a fundamental principle of Selective Networking that I want to emphasize – If one is actually networking, and not simply moving through the room marketing to everyone, a great deal of the selection takes care of itself. Let's look at some examples:

"Hi, I'm Sherill, 'Nature's Designs' custom jewelry. What an unusual necklace! I see you're wearing a service pin. I was with the Soroptimists before I moved, and I'd love to get involved with the community here. Are there several volunteer organizations in the area?"

Here I have introduced myself and given three seconds of my elevator pitch. I've indicated that we might have something in common since she is wearing what looks like a custom-made necklace. Then I let her know that I noticed something unrelated to a desire to make money, namely her service pin, and ask for some information about my new city. When she responds, selectivity comes into play. She might say:

"Hi, I'm Cindy, with A&M Realty. Custom jewelry? We could become best friends! Yes, we have lots of volunteer groups, and we're always looking for new members. I'm with the Rotary Club, let me introduce you to some people."

Or she might say:

"Hi, I'm Cindy, with A&M Realty. Let me give you, my card. The QR code will pull up several great listings available right now. It's a buyer's market."

Response "A" merits more conversation. Response "B" merits an exchange of cards and a graceful goodbye. In the first conversation, Cindy gave me a brief glimpse of her business, then heard and responded to what I said. We can see how the definition of networking: "A process of interacting with others in order to build rapport, exchange information and develop lasting connections.," is already underway. In the second conversation, Cindy is marketing to me while I am trying to network with her. It is possible that at another time Cindy will be in the networking head space. But at this moment, Selective Networking says, "Move on."

We have seen four situations in which we can interact long enough with someone for Selective Networking to suggest moving on. There is the cost factor (BMW) can the person afford what we have to offer? Then there is the relevance factor (Anti-aging skincare for the eighteen-year-old) does the person need what we have to offer? There is the philosophy factor (leather goods for the vegan) does the person want what we have to offer? Lastly, is the person listening, so she can interact with us?

Remember the popular saying, "Strive to be interested, rather than interesting." It is easy when we are tired, or anxious about business or facing a month-end crunch, to stop interacting with others and start marketing to them. But when we do, we lose our ability to listen and to be selective. We end up losing time, money, and lasting connections.

QUESTIONS FOR CONSIDERATION:

What is my mission statement?

Am I building a brand?

What plans should I have?

How much time do I have to devote to networking to build my business?

Am I being selective, and do I view networking as a sorting game?

Dr. Mikki St. Germain (h.c.)

Evolving Beyond Business Cards

Networking, evolving beyond business cards, awkward silence, and one-sided self-promotion.

Awkward. If that's what you think when attending a network event, it's time to switch gears and see it as an opportunity to build new relationships that will enhance and build your business.

If you are perceiving networking events, consisting of a room full of people wearing poorly placed name tags desperately trying to make a great first impression, handing off their business card and wait with bated breath for the phone to ring with that big break for their business, it's time to rethink and evolve into a better and more productive way to network.

Whether you love it or loathe it, networking is a necessity, and the importance of having professional contacts cannot be underestimated. However, there is a strong criterion that needs to be in place when building a business. – A symbiotic relationship!!

Whether it be business or personal, no one enjoys a one-sided relationship that makes us feel used and undervalued. There is a fine line in networking that can leave you feeling this way. Or worse, we may be doing things to others without realizing it. Let me share this thought, what do you think the other person is feeling when we do our five-minute pitch, hand them a business card and move on to the next person. We have limited time to network with a room full of people. We've all done it, standing there smiling as the person presenting their business is talking, the sound of their voice fades behind that voice in our heads asking, "is this person going to do business with me?" Stop thinking like that and start asking yourself, how can I do business with this person, so we create a symbiotic relationship and be an asset to each other?

It really is all about quality not quantity.

As with any relationship, communication, listening, supporting, and finding the common denominator is the key for successfully building a long-term relationship. I know many of you reading this may be asking.

"How can I find a common denominator when that person's business is not even in the same category as mine?"

That my friend is the opportunity!!! I'll give you an example. I met two women, both business owners at a networking event. One sold jewelry and the other was a health coach. At the time I was a martial arts instructor teaching men, women, and children. Out of a sea of people I had networked with at that event, I spent the rest of my time connecting with the two of them. I asked about their businesses. How did they reach new clients, and what did they offer as an incentive? Would they be willing to collaborate and cross our client base? By the end of the night, we had exchanged numbers, had a date on the calendar for the following week to meet and a plan to organize an event together. We titled it "Jewelry, Ju Jitsu and a Healthier You" Empowering women to be beautiful inside and out.

Each one of us invited our existing client base, along with marketing our event on through our own social media platforms. I saved money by networking and bartering the space for our event. I reached out to one of the martial arts studios that was centrally located for all three of us. I offered free advertising of his location as we marketed our event. Our event was 3 hours.

I taught women self-defense for 90 minutes; the health coach spoke and had an open forum for an hour and the jewelry was on display and had 30 minutes to speak and share her product.

We had over fifty-five women attend with the collaboration of invites between the three of us and our individual marketing. My students bought jewelry and booked her to be at other events. Many of my students connected with the health coach to enhance the benefits of weight loss as they were training with me in the martial arts. And as for me. I booked five outside women self-defense seminars from the clients they brought. Many of them wanted to enroll their children at the studio we were in. Which was perfect, as it enhanced the agreement, I made with the studio owner. Allowing me to have my event at his location was free advertising for his location. The whole event was a win/win scenario for all of us!

Networking is about building relationships where we help each other succeed.

Anyone who has studied martial arts knows there are benefits outside of kicking and punching. In the style I learned we had five principles that we needed to follow: effort, etiquette, sincerity, self-control, and character. Regardless of the martial arts these principles really apply to business. No business can succeed without effort, your effort is going to overflow into every facet of your business. You are going to spend countless hours fine tuning, building, and marketing yourself. Your etiquette is how your business is portrayed and remembered, is your product trustworthy? Sincerity is crucial, be honest, offer a true benefit that can make someone's life a little easier, a little better. Self-Control; learn to respond not react. Take responsibility for your business. Your character: you are your business! People will remember you for the little extra you do for them and genuinely mean it. Everyone you connect with will remember you one way or another.

We can all think of that one person we tend to avoid as the plague. I have a woman I met at a networking event five years ago contact me at least once a month to attend her events. While I appreciate her tenacity and follow-up, I have no intention of working with her. Why? In all the years I have known her, she has never asked me once about my business. Every conversation is directed toward her and her business. One sided relationship is a waste of time in the networking world.

If you are looking to succeed, be the person at networking events that everyone flocks to. Set the precedence that are you there to enhance another's business and create success together!

When I created KeepOnSharing, that is exactly what I had in mind as a social media platform.

We only succeed if you succeed. It's not like the traditional one-sided social media platforms where you are doing all the work by posting content, videos and ads and they reap all the benefits. I wanted a platform that breaks tradition and allows both of us to make money. Every social media platform makes billions of dollars off your content and your data. Everyone thought I was crazy to offer back 50% of the revenue on a social media platform with our users. My thought is if you are helping me to succeed, why wouldn't I share back the revenue? After all your time, content and videos are what helped me to build my business. KeepOnSharing is my way of creating a symbiotic relationship on a grander scale. – You're not just our customer, you're our partner" that is our business model.

Things only happen outside our comfort zone. Whether it be growing your business or networking. You have to take the time and listen, learn from each other, understand how the person you want to connect with approaches things. Are they the type of person who is knowledge-based, needing to know everything about it before they engage? They could be emotionally driven, where they want to feel good about themselves or know that what you have to offer gives back to the community. Networking is a "people" event, we are interacting with individuals who want to succeed just as much as you do. Think of how successful we can be when we do it together! Share your gift, defeat every obstacle, collaborate with others, and do what seems impossible and make it your reality!

"It's kind of fun doing the impossible," Walt Disney – Yes, it is Walt, yes, it is!!

QUESTIONS FOR CONSIDERATION:

What is my Why?

Is networking a necessity for me? If not? Why not?

How do I feel when I first enter a room with strangers?

Am I willing to collaborate with someone for a symbiotic relationship?

Can I think of different ways to improve my relationships in my networking world?

Dr. Vivian A. Haire (h.c.)

There is Room In The World For Every Great Gift

I heard something recently that caught my attention:

"The most you can do is all you can do, so just do it." Anonymous

In the scripture, Proverbs 31, It tells of the woman that does good and not evil all the days of her life. She rises up early and works willingly with her hands to supply food for her family. With her hands she plants a vineyard; she girded her loins with strength and strengthened her arms. She works deep into the night. She makes sure that her merchandise is good. She is not afraid to share with her maidens. And she reaches forth to the needy. For all that she works for she makes sure they are clothed with scarlet. She dresses herself in silk and purple. For strength and honor is her clothing. She opens her mouth with wisdom; and in her tongue is the law of kindness. Her children rise up and call her blessed; her husband also, and he praised her.

As I searched within myself, about being a virtuous and victorious woman, this scripture spoke to me. Whether you are single or a wife much is required in order to reach these goals. You have to stay connected! You must build a community!

When reaching out to others first, make sure that you have the correct contact information on those you are contacting. Make sure you're not sending out personal information. Only send out legitimate information and follow the laws within the media that you are using. Because there are so many scammers and ways of being scammed, it's important to keep them from knowing your personal information. Give them a challenge by changing your passwords frequently. There is nothing worse for someone you know than receiving a text or email from someone else, claiming to be you.

One: You must be willing to love and pursue, to accept the good and the bad. There will be times when you want to quit and throw in the towel. There will be times when you will ask yourself, what am I doing here? Am I crazy? I just don't have the money or the time. I don't know enough people. We all have the same 24 hours in the day, 1440 minutes, 86,400 seconds; it's what we do with our time that counts. Tell yourself you're not crazy, maybe you don't have the funds yet, but you still have the time, there are still people you have not even met yet. If you find yourself with only 10 or 20 followers, make them feel important and give them the best A-1 service you have. So, stay focused, stay on the course. I've always been told "good things come to those who wait" Lord gives me the patience to wait! It may not come when you want it, but somehow, someway it will come to you, right on time. Please don't sell yourself short. Stand tall and be counted, as long as you can move, breathe, walk, speak, think on good thoughts you are an important body in this world. It's sometimes necessary to encourage yourself when no one else does. So go ahead and encourage yourself. Don't become fearful if you hear others speaking negatively about you, you must be doing something right, otherwise people will not care or talk about you. You must be doing it right!

Two: You must be willing to seek after ways and sometimes stay up late hours in the night, and many times rising up early while it's still night. Thinking of ways to beautify and make it a one of a kind of business to please yourself and others business. You want to be able to impact people, giving a reason to share why they do business with you. Remember it's not always about how much money you can make. What matters is the relationship you build with the client and the quality of the service you offered. Recently, I had to reconsider sending a tiny brush to a customer, who was expecting a bigger brush. She would have been mad, if she had seen what she really ordered off the catalog page. People will not appreciate knowing what your monetary gains are. What they care about is how you treat them. It would be wise to make them feel good so that they can refer to you and also be a loyal customer.

Many times, your own family will not support or help by giving you a kind word or even supporting you a tiny bit. For one day you may be able to allow them to see you were serious if you work hard and have that desire to be pleasing. Keep pushing forward and be of good cheer. Forget the naysayers, it is your business, not theirs. Sometimes your blessing will come in ways you could never see coming. Believe in yourself and your goals. Have faith and believe in your self-worth. I recall a great spoken line in a movie, "A shoe is just a shoe until someone steps into it" Do you plan to walk in your own shoes or someone else's? We must all learn to carry our own and walk the road of our own success or failure. No one wants to fail, but when you do, don't be fearful or cause anything to feel you can't get up and try again. I encourage you as I encourage myself. Dust off the dust and start again! Some of our most successful businesses and entrepreneurs have failed more than once but they got back up again. The important thing here is to learn from your mistakes!

Three: Always allow kind and positive words out of your mouth; for this is what makes a lasting impression on others. We all have or need something from each other. Sometimes it can take half a lifetime before we discover that we are interdependent.

Fourth and final: Don't think yourself greater and better than anybody else. There is room in the world for every great gift. We all have been given our own personal and original God given gifts. I personally have always felt that if we all do good with what God gave us to do, there would be no room for jealousy. The internet for instance, I feel has its positive and sometimes negative influence. Just think if you spread positive vibes into the atmosphere, it can sometimes touch people where the need is needed most. Every day we wake up is another day to share with someone your gift that you were blessed to bring forth into the world. Just sitting down and putting pen to paper was a challenge for me. But I was challenged, and others close to me trusted me to write. I jumped out of my comfort zone. My community, my Village, my connections in a Wonderful Network enabled me to express myself on paper, Something I never was convinced I could ever do. This was indeed a challenge! The conclusion is a feeling of great accomplishment. No one knows their future but chooses to make your life worth living. Once you conquer FEAR, you'll find comfort and calmness through the storm. Just take it step by step and move in the right direction. For you have the victory and victory is yours.

QUESTIONS FOR CONSIDERATION:

How am I staying connected?

Have I stayed focused and connected with people I met months before? Why or Why not?

How can I stay focused on retaining past customers and still grow my business?

How can I help them without feeling pushy?

How can I build a better relationship with my community?

Dr. Felicia Harris (h.c.)

Referrals, An Important Lifeline To Your Business

As a business owner, why ask for referrals? Referrals are an important lifeline to your business. I am going to share with you many techniques for getting referrals. Hopefully, this will take your referral game to the next level.

I have four types of referrals.

1. Warm chatter referrals. This type of referral is when I am out warm- chattering. For many this is the most feared. I am out purposely meeting new and unfamiliar people with the anticipation of finding a new customer through a warm conversation. Because you are meeting a total stranger, the fear of rejection sets in. But for me, I love the challenge. In fact, if I get a "No," I thank them. The person is often taken by surprise and curious as to why I thanked them. I say, because I wanted to see how many "No's" I received before I actually had someone say

"Yes." It is important that when asking for a referral is to build a relationship and trust with the person that I am asking for the referral. After all, you are asking this person to give you the name and contact number of their family members, friends, coworkers, neighbors, church members, etc....

2. Referrals from my Mary Kay party. This type of referral is easier, in my opinion, because I am able to obtain names and phone numbers at the party. I have already established a relationship, earned the trust, and pampered the ladies. I incorporate in obtaining referral by playing the referral game. The first customer that completes their list of at least ten names and phone numbers wins an amazing Mary Kay Skin Care or Glamour product. Of course, everyone is a winner!

3. Referrals from businesses. This type of referral is from my connection with business partners, such as my local Temecula Valley Chamber of Commerce, Menifee Community Partners, community groups and organizations. Often times this referral may be spontaneous during a conversation. I would say that this is the easiest way to get referrals. This is a great connection. Join organizations that support its members. Attend as many events as possible. It is important to be visible, after all you are building your brand.

4. Referrals from existing clients. Create a referral program. This will help with a steady stream of clients. Referrals bring new customers. You can decide what gift you want to give to your existing clients for giving you

referrals. Gift cards are always a great choice. If you have provided great customer service and experience, word of mouth referrals is an added value.

It is important to have business cards and samples of your product. With your business cards, my suggestion is to have a professional photo taken for your cards. Many potential customers will keep a business card with a photo versus a business card without a photo.

Just as important as obtaining referrals, it is equally important to track your referrals. There are many services that you can use to input the referral names information in a database. You may want to consider a paid service that allows you to send text messages and emails with just a few clicks from your computer.

In conclusion, it is always best to be just authentic when speaking to new prospects. Have great eye contact and if they are comfortable and extend a handshake.

QUESTIONS FOR CONSIDERATION:

How do you handle rejection?

Are you willing to incentivize your captured audience?

How do you propose to do this?

How do you track your referrals

Do you have a business card? Is it Virtual or Traditional?

Do you know what a QR code is? How do you get the information from it?

Dr. Raven L. Hilden (h.c.)

Networking Through Volunteering

Volunteering is a fulfilling experience that can bring a sense of purpose and satisfaction to your life. You get to make a positive impact on the lives of others and the community, and you also have the opportunity to learn new skills and expand your network. Networking is an essential part of any career or business, and volunteering provides a unique opportunity to make new connections with like-minded individuals. In this chapter, we will explore the benefits of networking while volunteering and how it can help you achieve your personal and professional goals.

As the Founder and CEO of MilVet, a nonprofit organization, I have witnessed life-changing transformations while serving our military families and also in our volunteers. Some have discovered new strengths and learned new skills. Others were connected to the right people at just the right time. Some found hope after they thought there was none. All have had a profound effect on the lives of others and experienced the true gift of giving. Here are a few of the many benefits of networking through volunteering.

1. Expand your network

Volunteering provides an excellent opportunity to meet new people and expand your network. You will meet people from different backgrounds, professions, and ages who share your passion for making a difference in the community. These connections can lead to new friendships and potential job or business opportunities in the future.

Not only are you sharing your experiences with your network, but you are also reaching the network of the nonprofits that you serve or donate to. This can dramatically expand your reach! Consider partnering with a nonprofit for an event by volunteering, sponsoring, or hosting an event and donating a portion to the organization. You can reach thousands of new people, thereby expanding your network and bottom line.

Volunteering can also help you build relationships with people who can offer you advice, mentorship, or connections to other professionals in your field. For example, if you are interested in pursuing a career in marketing, volunteering at a non-profit organization that focuses on marketing can help you meet professionals in this field who can guide you on your career path. You have the potential to meet local leaders, industry experts, potential clients and more.

Your network can also connect you to new friendships and partnerships with others who have the same heart for giving back. I have made so many quality friendships through volunteer work and so have many others.

2. Improve your job prospects

Volunteering can enhance your job prospects by providing you with new skills and experiences that can make you more attractive to potential employers. Employers value candidates who have demonstrated a commitment to community service and have developed transferable skills such as teamwork, leadership, and problem-solving.

Volunteering can also help you gain relevant experience in a particular field, which can be valuable when applying for jobs. For example, if you are interested in working in the healthcare industry, volunteering at a hospital or clinic can provide you with hands-on experience and help you build relationships with healthcare professionals. Volunteer experience is great for resumes and many organizations are happy to write a letter of recommendation for you to speak on your character and contributions to the team and community.

3. Learn new skills

Volunteering can provide you with opportunities to learn new skills that can be useful in your personal and professional life. You can learn leadership, communication, and organizational skills by volunteering in a leadership position, working on a committee or coordinating events.

Getting involved in nonprofit organizations can also provide you with opportunities to learn technical skills such as web design, social media marketing, or data analysis. Many non-profit organizations need volunteers with these skills to help them reach their goals, and volunteering can be a great way to gain practical experience in these areas. Nonprofits also need fundraisers, caseworkers, field representatives, accountants, office managers, program leads and much more.

4. Develop your personal brand

Volunteering can help you develop your personal brand by demonstrating your commitment to community service and your passion for a particular cause. This can be valuable when building your personal brand online or networking with professionals in your field.

For example, real estate agents might want to partner with a nonprofit that provides housing, banks can host financial workshops with nonprofits to reach more folks who can benefit from their services.

Perhaps you are a financial advisor and are passionate about reducing poverty. You could consider partnering with a nonprofit to host a financial literacy workshop. Your brand would reflect your expertise in the field and dedication to supporting your community. Your brand can make you stand out when someone is looking for financial services. These events are great content to share on social media or in press releases for more visibility.

Supporting a nonprofit or cause in your community is a remarkable thing to share! This helps the nonprofit obtain more support, brings awareness to the cause, and helps connect you to likeminded partners or clients. Besides, folks love to hear about good things and will be more receptive to your marketing!

5. Improve Mental Health and Wellbeing

Giving back to the community provides benefits to the community and recipients, and to you as well. It is an opportunity to see the world from a different lens. One of our volunteers with MilVet, a veteran, was grieving the loss of a loved one and had a tough time interacting with others. He became despondent and lonely. We convinced him to help us distribute gifts to families in need for the holidays. This was during covid, and we met a grandmother to provide gifts to her and her 12-year-old grandson. The grandfather had stage 4 cancer due to his service in Vietnam and the medical bills caused them to lose their home. When we delivered the gifts, the grandmother was in tears and our volunteer saw that he was able to bring some joy to another person struggling with difficulties as well.

Far too many veterans I have met struggle with a sense of purpose post-military. However, veterans are not the only ones who need a sense of belonging and purpose. Getting involved in causes that move you can provide a powerful way to make a positive difference in the community and quite possibly the world!

6. Bring Joy to Your Life

Volunteering reduces stress! Experts report that when you focus on someone other than yourself, it interrupts usual tension-producing patterns.

Many volunteer organizations and projects provide fun as well. MilVet volunteers help with live concerts, attend award ceremonies, plan holiday events for children, participate in parades and so much more! We all have a different idea of fun and there is surely something for everyone. Many nonprofits are good at recognizing volunteers and making sure that your contributions are appreciated.

Helpful tip - remember to follow up! Networking as a volunteer provides numerous advantages but they only work if you connect with those you meet. One of the biggest mistakes you can make is failure to reach out to your network and establish a relationship with them. Make a list during or after your event with the names of those you want to follow up with. Jot notes on the back of their business card or schedule it on the calendar on your phone.

Now that you know of some of the many advantages of volunteering, where do you start? There are nonprofit networking groups that can connect you to many organizations so you can give to multiple causes and find a few that you are truly passionate about. This is a great way to learn more about nonprofits, network, and support others - even if you only attend one meeting a month. If you already know of a particular cause you are passionate about, reach out to the organization directly or visit your local Chamber of Commerce website for a list of nonprofits. If you are looking to give back to veterans and their families, please visit www.milvet.org.

The advantages of volunteering can be immense. It can help expand your network, improve job prospects, learn new skills, develop your brand, improve your well-being, and bring joy to your life! Your contributions will be an incredible benefit to local organizations, those they serve and even more for you personally and professionally. I wish you an abundance of happiness, love, and success in your journeys!

QUESTIONS FOR CONSIDERATION:

Where can I find a list of non-profits?

How can I benefit from Volunteering, Am I just paying it forward?

What organization could benefit from my knowledge?

Kristie Jacobo

Why Leave Money On The Table

Have you ever received an invitation to a high school reunion? A message pops up in your inbox reading "Class of 1997 20-year reunion" and your stomach drops. Immediately, emotions start firing from every cylinder. Fear, anxiety, elation, and excitement are all rushing through your veins. You start to over analyze the event that is still six months ahead. Why does this happen?

It is human nature to remember events in our lives that stimulate our emotions. We might not remember a password that we reset yesterday, but we remember how we felt that day twenty years ago when the popular boy complimented our dress in science class. Most of us can remember exactly where we were when the planes crashed into the Twin Towers. We remember popular jingles from commercials or lyrics to songs that we have not heard in years. Yet, we introduce ourselves to someone at a conference, walk away, and think to ourselves, what was that person's name again? This happens when the interaction lacks emotional connection.

We are engrained with the idea that we must master our elevator speech. The thought is that if we have only thirty seconds with someone in an elevator, we must have the ability to effectively communicate a sales pitch to entice that individual to want to learn more about our business. What a bunch of rubbish! We spend countless hours in sales training courses on this so-called elevator moment. The plan is narcissistic at best. We don't gain sales opportunities by riding in elevators, hoping for thirty seconds to spit out a sales pitch about ourselves. If that is the case, we might as well just leave money on the table.

The cultural school of thought in America is "What's in it for me?" People are not generally invested in what others are doing if they do not see a benefit for themselves. There needs to be an emotional connection, an answer to a personal need. To be successful in business, we must understand how to establish this connection. Instead of the elevator speech, we need to spend the first thirty seconds finding a personal connection or something we have in common. People love to talk about themselves. So let them. Then find a common ground to respond about. Chances are we will remember their name and can determine how we can benefit them with our product or service.

Let's go back to the high school reunion for a minute. Imagine that when you arrive, you recognize some faces that you can't recall the names for. There are two options here: Either you avoid the person all night because you are embarrassed that you forgot their name, or you approach the individual and share a laugh about the group project you two worked on in math class during your junior year. Next, you see the girl who lived in poverty, so you avoid talking to her because you assume there is still nothing in common. Later that evening, she is introduced to you with a doctorate prefix. Trust me, this is a name you won't forget.

Building a network begins with our authentic behavior. True, there are some people who have mastered the "fake it 'til you make it" philosophy. In general, however, that lack of integrity will catch up at some point and have a negative impact on their reputation. Spending time on sales pitches comes across as gimmicky and phony. When we are a product of our product, a result of a service we provide, it's easy to relay the authenticity of the benefit. When we believe we have the answer to a problem, we portray sincerity. Most importantly, when we consistently prove that our intention is not a hot sale, but a desire to benefit others, we will generate success through network referrals.

A critical component to sales and network is recognizing that our audience and our customers are constantly evolving. A fundamental error is the assumption that we know who not to approach. We don't talk to the girl who lived in poverty, because we know that she cannot afford our product. We don't initiate contact with a person about our skin care line because we heard her husband recently passed and She has other issues to deal with.

We don't offer a financial consult to a friend because we assume He wants to keep His finances private. We don't take advantage of creating a social medial reel because we think our friends and family will tease us. These assumptions are what is holding us back.

Building our version of the American Dream will look different to each one of us. Finding confidence and overcoming insecurities is not easy. Stepping outside of comfort zone is scary. But living in our comfort zone is even more frightening. Learning to exempt judgement allows us the freedom to be unapologetic about our authentic selves. Children are incredible at this. They put on a cape and believe they can fly. If we can adopt this mindset in our business actions, we can fly too. Instead of leaving money on the table, we need to leave our doubts and our inhibitions on the table. We need to rid ourselves of assumptions and judgements and free ourselves of the fears that hold us back from reaching our potential. The Law of Attraction lends to the belief that if we manifest the person we intend to become, our actions will naturally lead us along that path.

We need to get to that place in our mind where we open the e-mail invitation for the next high school reunion and think "I can't wait to reconnect." We show up and reintroduce ourselves, feeling confident about the person we are today and who we intend to become in the future. This is the liberating moment we dream of. When we choose to make an emotional connection with our authentic selves, we become unstoppable. We stop apologizing for asking tough questions. Rejection does not offend us. We become believable and passionate in our network. Fearless and non-judgmental are the new pillars of our communication. When all is said and done, the only thing welcome at our table is another chair.

QUESTIONS FOR CONSIDERATION:

Is there a desire to benefit others or myself?

What happens when my interaction lacks emotional connection?

Do I allow my new prospects to talk about themselves by taking control of the conversation? Why or Why not?

What am I leaving on the table because I am living in my comfort zone?

Am I judging the other person by either their appearance, actions, or both?

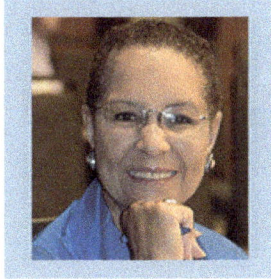

Carol Latham

Timing, Trust, & Attitude

TIMING

"One day when you look back, you will understand that everything happens for a reason. What is meant for you will be yours at the right time." C.S. Lewis

Over the years, we may experience times when we realize it was necessary to let go and let God guide the way. We need that to be the benchmark. It's important that while waiting, planning on, or working for the 'right and fruitful time' to remember to make the most of the present time.

We are all under pressure to be more, to do more and to keep on top of our responsibilities. But at every turn we must remind ourselves of who we are and why we are here, so we can keep above the fray. We must hold a positive vision of what we want for ourselves and others and keep our thoughts, words, and actions in harmony with our vision.

We often hear that timing is everything. So, it is important to understand that making the right decision in any area of your life at the right time can make a tremendous difference that requires patience and effort.

Timing in business is critical to ensure the prompt execution of projects, the pivoting of strategies, launching of services or products by entrepreneurs. In order not to miss opportunities, these decisions all require careful consideration of market trends, consumer needs and competition.

In personal relationships, timing can affect the outcome of many important life events, for example marriage proposals, starting a family, changing jobs and, more.

Waiting in the wings while being and persistence can pay off. So, doing the work, keeping your skills fresh in preparation for the right time, being patient and finding the many ways that will aid in making better decisions will lead to success at the right time.

TRUST

"Trust is earned when actions meet words." Chris Butler

Trust isn't something to take lightly. We all want relationships, whether personal or business, built on a strong foundation of trust. In fact, it should be the benchmark for all relationships. Trust can be the one element that brings people together or tears them apart.

Trust is a valuable asset and the foundation of mutual respect, understanding, and honesty, which is necessary for all meaningful interaction to happen. Trust allows for an openness

of feelings and vulnerability. However, once trust is broken, it can cause irreparable damage.

Trusting implies a reliance on the other person to do what they say they will do. That they will 'walk their talk' and fulfill their commitments whether in a personal relationship or in business. Trust is essential to cultivate, nurture and maintain a healthy environment of trustworthiness to ensure meaningful and successful relationships.

ATTITUDE

"A positive attitude gives you power over your circumstances instead of your circumstances having power over you." Joyce Meyer

Daily we must renew and review our attitude. This is essential – a fundamental aspect of our daily life as it shapes our thoughts, behavior, and emotions. By doing this we can keep the negative thoughts and actions away.

Our attitude and mindset means everything because it is our personal point of view. Our personal road map, the consciousness that guides our life. Thankfully, it is this consciousness that will guide our lives if we let it.

At every turn we must remind ourselves of who we are and why we are here, so we can keep above the fray. We must hold a positive vision of what we want for ourselves and others and

keep our thoughts, words, and actions in harmony with that vision.

Let us determine our core values, beliefs, and practice gratitude, mindfulness, compassion, and kindness in our daily lives. Use them when we speak to yourself in words of strong affirmation. Add faith and visualization to them. This one daily activity done consistently is a powerful tool. The right attitude can help us overcome challenges, lead a rewarding, fulfilling life and achieve our wildest dreams.

If there is one of these tenets that surpasses the others, it would be Trust. Trust is the foundation in any relationship, especially the one we have with ourselves. It is what enables us to trust when timing is right and if it isn't that we can overcome the challenges presented. It is trust that encourages us to have a positive attitude because we know that with a good, positive attitude we can handle all that confronts us.

"Trust in the timing of everything that happens and allow a positive attitude to encourage your growth." Anonymous

Carol Latham

Projecting Professional Image With Personal Style

We each have an IMAGE. However, we are, however we present ourselves to others defines the Image that they have of us. We communicate in every aspect of our lives often without saying a word. We all want to look attractive, well put together, polished, and professional, but sometimes we need a little guidance, reassurance, or a nudge in the better direction. The 12 steps herein will explore some of these. Keep in mind we are looking for a TOTAL package not just one aspect on its own.

"A strong positive self-image is the best possible preparation for success." Joyce Brothers

FIRST IMPRESSION - You only get one chance to make a first impression

Statistics state that more than half of a first impression is based upon looks and body language. Research confirms that within seconds of first meeting someone, we start to make up our minds about them.

Since you have only seconds in which to make this first impression, at this first glance you'll want your appearance to register, followed quickly by a friendly smile, confident posture, steady eye contact, and great attitude. These all combine to make up your Professional Image – the way that others see you.

The more professional your image, the more others will want to know you and do business with you. Remember that people will be more apt to do business with people they know, like and trust.

We are judged upon these ten elements:

1. Economic Level

2. Educational Level

3. Trustworthiness

4. Social Position.

5. Level of Sophistication

6. Moral Character.

7. Level of Success

8. Social Heritage

9.   Educational Heritage

10. Economic Heritage.

So, what message do you want to communicate about yourself to your peers, associates, boss, clients, or people in general? Do you communicate professionalism and seriousness about the work you do, and do you command respect and confidence in your abilities and position?

The reason why your individuality is so important is because it communicates creativity and leadership potential. It demonstrates a knowledge of who you are, confidence in yourself and your abilities. This image building takes practice, consistency, and experimentation.

1. ENTRANCE AND EXITS:

There is a psychology of making a good first and last impression when you enter or exit a room. Are you rushing in out of breath perhaps due to being late or confidently filling the doorway and making your presence noticed?

2. POSTURE, WALK AND BODY MOTIONS:

The way you sit, and stand is the first crucial influence on other's first impression of you. It tells about your self-confidence, approachability, attitude and your respect for others and yourself.

Is your body posture one of inclusiveness allowing others to join in or is it passive, slouched, or assertive?

Correct stance: Stand tall with back straight. Are your arms folded across your chest in a protective, bored posture or are you just cold?

Sitting position: Sit upright with arms and legs relaxed.

Reflective Body Language: Imitating the movement of another person.

Optimal Distance: How close do you like to stand/ sit with someone else. Test your own optimal distance: make eye contact with someone walking towards you. Stop when you are no longer comfortable. The usual intimate space is 0-18" personal is 18" – 4', social is 4' – 12' and public distance is 12'+

WALK AND BODY MOTION: You want your walk to demonstrate confidence by holding your head high, chest lifted, arms and legs moving easily in unison, and having a measured stride that is neither too short nor too long without any shuffling of feet.

There are four motion types:

a) emblems-nods of agreement, smiles for pleasantness.

b) illustrators-support of a point e.g., a fist in victor.

c) adapters-which enables us to deal with uneasiness, nervous tapping of fingers, playing with hair, etc.

d) regulators or movements - eye contact indicates interest.

3. EYE CONTACT AND FACIAL EXPRESSIONS:

The expression 'the eyes are the windows of the soul' is very true. The face and the way the eyes and eyebrows are used are the most expressive parts of our bodies. They enable us to have rapport with others and it can make or break you. Make it one of sincerity. Be aware that culturally, eye contact is permissible in some cultures and discouraged in others. So read the total package. We, of course, avoid eye contact when it is convenient e.g., to avoid being singled out in class or not tipping our hand when playing poker, etc.

Eye contact types:

- Wanda / Wally Wanderer: is indicative of boredom, disinterest.

- Doris / Donald Downcaster: more feminine, sensual, coy, untrustworthy, disrespect in some cultures,

- Sarah / Sammy Starer: ogling, uncomfortable, bold, aggressive.

- Rachel / Richard Relaxed: attentive, interested, receptive.

Facial Expressions:

What does our facial expression say about us? Make it a look of sincerity, enthusiasm, interest, and positivity.

The six basic emotions are happiness, sadness, anger, disgust, surprise, and fear. The most welcoming of these being the smile of happiness. Keep it in your voice when on the phone, the result will be more pleasant and friendly. Try standing when you make calls too as it changes the physicality of your presentation. Use a mirror to help you keep aware of your expressions throughout the day. Remember, sometimes our words say one thing, but our expression indicates another. Have you ever tried telling a sad story with a happy face? It is difficult to do!

4. GESTURES: This is vital to communicating thoughts, feelings, and ideas. Gestures involve various parts of the body and should not be taken out of context without consideration to other body signals. They are NOT universal as a gesture acceptable here may not be somewhere else.

Gestures are commonly perceived as warm or cold. Warm gestures may be leaning towards people when speaking or listening, smiling, touching, and expressively gesturing. Examples of Cold gestures are hands on hips, slouching, no eye contact, lack of smiles. Nervous gestures include - biting, cleaning fingernails, fidgeting, etc.

Examples of Gestures and what they may mean:

- Rubbing hands together - excitement or acquiescence

- Fiddling with change in pocket - indicates money concerns

- Clenched hands - hostility

- Steeple shaped upwards hands - dominance over

listener /downwards - listening

- Clasping hands behind your back - authority (policemen, etc.)

- Covering mouth with hand - lacking self-confidence.

- Touching or rubbing nose - deceit.

- Supporting head when listening - boredom, sleepy

- Picking at imaginary lint - boredom

- Hands on hips - readiness and aggressiveness. Legs apart increases this.

5. APPEARANCE: - Style of Dress:

Clothing acts as a communicator of ourselves, our company, and our position. Ask yourself what kind of image do you want? What message do you communicate about yourself to peers, colleagues, associates, and the higher managers/directors in the clothing you wear?

Dressing appropriately for an interview increases your hiring or upward possibilities. 75% of the decision to hire is based on the applicant's appearance. Wrinkles, soiled, unpolished shoes, etc. won't make the cut. Within 2 - 3 seconds we are sized up. This happens very unconsciously. A pleasing appearance can of course boost your self-confidence.

What are some of the appearance elements? Build your wardrobe around what you already own.

- Get organized - organize your closet. Remove what hasn't been worn in a year. You must have an appropriate workable wardrobe. Group your clothes in type.

- Select a color scheme you are comfortable with. Build it around solid neutrals then work in patterns and prints.

- Invest in classics - think quality and fit.

- Buy the best you can afford - select quality over quantity. Most expensive does not mean better quality neither does a designer label!

- Choose year-round fabrics - wool gabardines - or other natural fibers and blends.

- Maintain your wardrobe - repair. have a good tailor to work on alterations and repairs.

- Tastefully use accessories - don't go overboard.

- Women: scarves, shoes, hosiery, glasses, handbags, jewelry, and belts.

- Men: good watch, ring, belt, ties, socks, and shoes.

- Pick a suitable and manageable hairstyle.

- Take care of your skin, suitable makeup, nails that are clean, tidy & shorter) and general hygiene are a part of the package.

- Individualize your professional image.

Hints: Business attire is NOT for extremes and conservative doesn't mean dowdy. It's always better to be over-dressed than under-dressed.

Seek out mentors with the image you like.

Follow what works for you, incorporate it into YOUR own style with confidence, authenticity, and self-assurance.

Women - Suitable shoes (pump) clean and in good condition - not too high or strappy for business.

Watch out for visible bra straps and underwear lines. If wearing a sheer blouse, wear a concealer underneath.

Pants should be looser in fit and lines.

Men: Basic (white, beige, and blue)shirt with an attractive tie always works the best.

Sensible clean shoes.

Best suit - pure wool or blend in blue, gray, or beige. The darker the suit the more authority it conveys. Use brown more sparingly and black conveys, funerals. Take your time shopping for a suit and go wearing the shirt, belt, and shoes you plan to wear with it.

Socks - match or closely match pants or shoes.

Hair and facial hair should be properly groomed.

If you use your vehicle for business, keep it clean inside

and out. The same tidiness applies to your briefcase. Keep it organized!

8. VOICE:

What are we conveying with our voices in person or on the telephone? Remember we make tremendous impact with our voice by:

- (a) TONE what is the inflection and how do we say things?

- (b) QUALITY is it nasal, harsh?

- (c) INTENSITY/LOUDNESS is it high pitched, baby soft and what does it say to/about us?

- (d) RATE do we speak too quickly or too slowly? What does that convey?

- (e) PAUSE remember to allow occasional pauses for emphasis.

- (f) VOCABULARY and GRAMMAR the use of proper grammar and vocabulary speaks volumes about our overall professionalism and image.

- (g) CONVERSATIONAL and LISTENING SKILLS Pay attention to what is being said and interact accordingly. Keep the smile in your voice!

9. INTRODUCTIONS: This is critical as we have about 4 minutes to make the impression that we are confident, warm, intelligent, etc.

Basic rules:

- introduce a man to woman
- younger to older
- lower rank to higher
- lesser known to more known
- peer in your company to peer of another
- fellow executive to customer or client
- nonofficial to official.

Use both names in introductions. Repeating the names is always helpful.

If you forget a name admit it without too much apology, if they forget yours supply it without embarrassing them and maybe remind them where you met before. Remember to use titles if they apply and stand for introductions. Always be courteous, tactful and project your most contagious, authentic quality through your smile.

To best represent yourself you should have a simple, interesting message that you are comfortable with to describe what you do. Your own personal '20 second elevator speech.'

10. HANDSHAKES:

A good handshake is positive, firmly held for about 3-4 seconds with direct eye contact. It can convey personal magnetism, confidence, and self-control. We all have met some of the following:

- Carlotta / Charley Cruncher: too overwhelming, trying too hard

- Fiona / Freddi Fish: limp wrist suggests timidity, disinterest.

- Carla / Carlos Common: clinging, holding too long, maybe placing one on top or holding forearm , which suggests control.

- Felicity / Freddie Friendly: good grip, warm, hearty, eye contact and 3-4 seconds.

11. BREATHING AND RELAXATION:

Boost your energy level and confidence by deep breathing and allowing the body to relax and find its own level of equilibrium.

12. COMMUNICATIONS:

The final check mark is how we follow up with people we meet. Thank you notes and letters of appreciation, congratulations, etc. are always appreciated and a way of making you memorable.

'We cannot become what we want by remaining what we are.'

Max Depree

If you want to be perceived as a professional that people will like, respect, and want to conduct business with, you need to present yourself in a manner that through your appearance, speech and mannerisms will best indicate that image.

QUESTIONS FOR CONSIDERATION:

When has waiting paid off for me?

When did I procrastinate and prevented myself from a great opportunity?

How do I feel when trust is broken? Can that ever be repaired?

What are my core values? List 5 most important values to you.

Have I benefited from being kind and supportive of others? What happened?

Do I have a positive vision of what I desire?

If so how well do I communicate that desire?

Dr. Tyara Lee (h.c.)

Entrepreneurship Is Not Fast Money

Every time you leave the house is a networking opportunity. Networking doesn't necessarily mean you are going to an event. When you are networking with someone you are simply interacting with others and exchanging information. Just complimenting someone's earrings and they ask you your name is a simple form of networking. Next time you leave your house I want you to be prepared with a nice goodie or gift bag, don't forget to include your business card inside. You should be ready to hand it to at least 1-3 people per day. The key is not to just hand them a business card and say hey this is my business follow me, but to develop a connection with them before sharing your business card.

Some may ask how can I network better if not a master at networking:

1. Know what your why is

2. Set goals of how many new contacts you would like to save

3. Know your target audience

4. Know that the person you are networking with may know someone who is interested in what you have to offer

5. Utilizing online platforms

6. Attend events

7. Be authentically you

8. Offer value & information

9. Be a problem solver (what problem does your product of service solve)?

10. Volunteer

11. Practice your "effective" listening skills

12. Follow up

13. Always keep a positive outlook no matter their response

14. Be sincere

15. Maintain strong relationship

16. Connect with people beyond your market or industry

17. Join networking groups

There are so many levels and ways to network. My very first-time networking was many years ago in elementary school, I gathered together an all-girls singing group. We went to lower-level classrooms to sing songs we rehearsed. This is a prime example of you are never too young or too old to network or start something great!

I believe that networking is the most important part of Entrepreneurship. Some people think entrepreneurship is fast money overnight when I'm in most cases it's a marathon not a sprint. You have got to network & build relationships. One of the fastest growing markets right now is social media.

You can network on social media in various ways. Social media is one of the best marketing platforms out there because they are mostly free!

My Social Media top 4 Platforms that are worth spending time on and growing your database & business with:

1. Tik Tok

2. Facebook

3. Instagram

4. YouTube

These platforms are free to download and capitalize on.

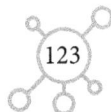

Here's the trick to possibly going viral.

1. Believe in yourself

2. Don't be afraid to network & meet strangers

3. Use popular hashtags /use your own

4. Post 3 times a day

5. Engagement posts

6. Reals / short video clips

7. Create informative content

8. High resolution videos & photos

9. Share your story

10. Post at the right times example (PST 4am, 9:00am, 3pm, 6pm) times may very

11. Create a flier of your post schedule or live schedule (Canva.com is free)

12. Use different content

13. Pay attention to the news or current popular events (use for post engagement or video engagement)

14. Email reminders of lives (constantcontact.com or even Wix.com) is great for building database

15. Text reminder of lives (loyaltyshops.com) is great.

There are so many other ways, but those are just a few to get you started. go viral on social media, but it's about what you do after you go viral. You got this! It's a process so stay focused & be consistent. I want you to know that you have the key to unlock the door to success.

QUESTIONS FOR CONSIDERATION:

Don't feel afraid to share your information. Why?

Are you using Social Media platforms to expand your business growth?

How many times per day are you posting?

What are the best times to post?

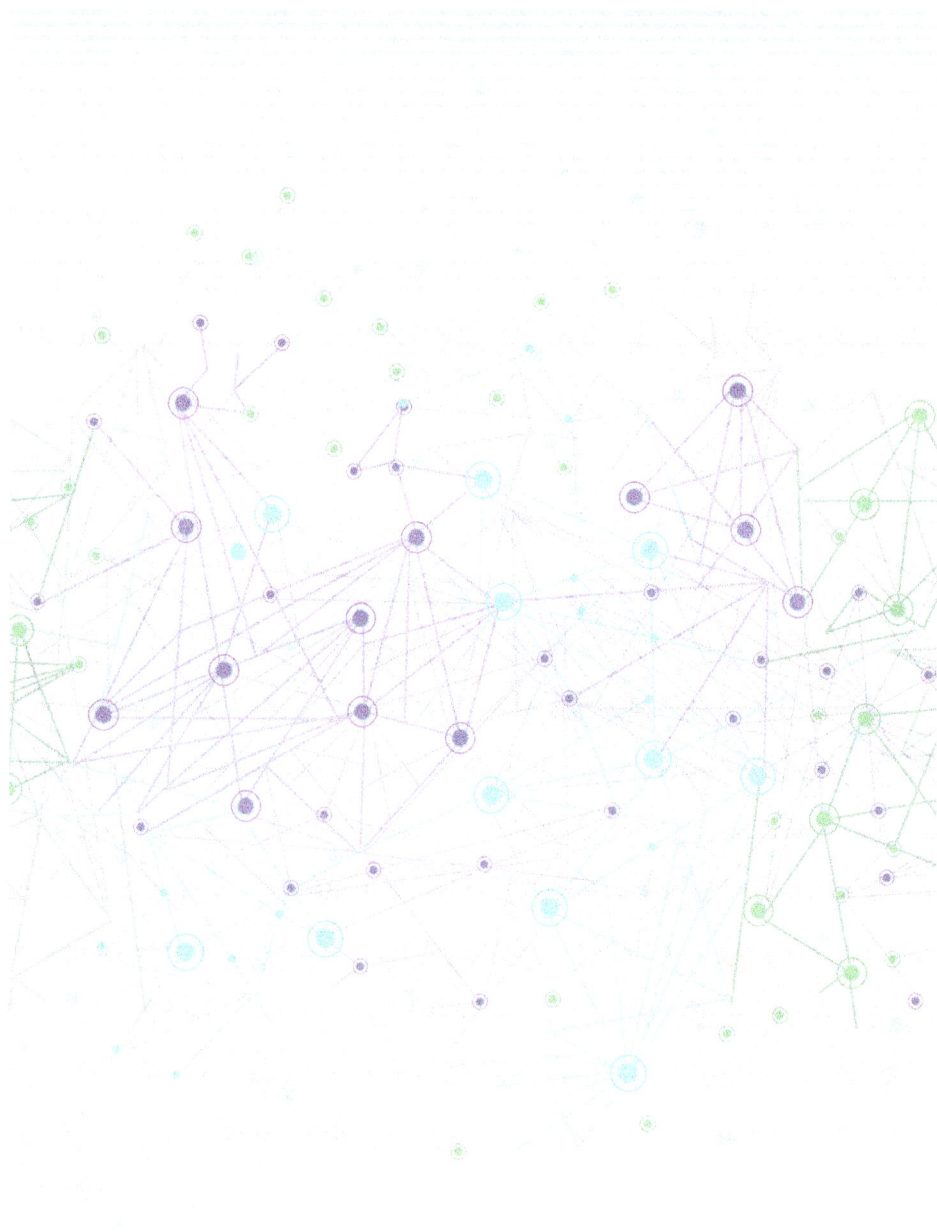

Dr. Jeannette LeHoullier (h.c.)

Networking Using Social Media

Have you thought about ways to reach family or friends that you have had no contact with for many years? You may be an entrepreneur looking for alternative options to promote your business. I enjoy connecting and **NETWORKING**, I have used many **SOCIAL MEDIA** outlets and options to create community and connectivity. Recently, I used my **Facebook** KCHS Alumni Private **GROUP** to plan my 50th Class Reunion.

If you are wondering why use Social Media, here are some reasons. Let us explore some ways that I have found Social Media to be effective and worthwhile. There are various platforms for this type of networking such as **Facebook, YouTube, Instagram, Twitter, Blogpost, LinkedIn, Pinterest, Alignable, Nextdoor,** etc. I do not claim to be an expert at platforms, so I will just share what has been successful in my personal and business life. We all have our opinions about the use of this way of marketing, connecting, and networking. For me, I have enjoyed the learning approach to my Social Media activity.

Facebook is one of the most known online Networking/ Social Media platforms. Most users create a profile and begin connecting with friends and family. It has been proven to be a wonderful way to communicate and keep current on activities of those we add as "Friends." However, let me share ways I have used Facebook features such as **GROUP, PAGE,** and **EVENTS**.

- A **GROUP** is an example of an effective way to network and connect while having a permanent site to reference over the years.

    o For example, I have enjoyed collecting various recipes posted on my Facebook newsfeed. I surmised that there must be an easier way to collect and save interesting recipes without long searches through years of posts by others.

    o I created a **GROUP** for saving and sharing recipes with my interested Facebook "Friends" and entitled it **"RECIPES from Facebook."**

        ▪ Private Link: https://www.facebook.com/ groups/1500940060187773/.

    o It has been an optional posting site that "Friends" can join.

    o Honestly, it has been a joy to share recipes over the

past 10 years.

o Eventually, I realized that I wanted to broaden my Recipe aficionado audience to include the Public by creating a Facebook PAGE.

- (See more information below under PAGES.)

- **I implemented the Family GROUP feature to create three private places to honor family.**

o After both my beloved (1) Grandma Grace and (2) Mother passed away, I created a NETWORKING way for family to connect to both individualized GROUPS to honor my loved ones. It helped the family stay closer and to share photos for wonderful memories.

o When my (3) youngest son had cancer, I set up a GROUP to honor him. Close family and his friends were able to support and encourage him as he went through surgery, chemotherapy, hospitalization, and recovery.

o Each Family GROUP has provided positive and encouraging outlets for personal networking and connection.

- **A Community GROUP is a**nother successful way for SOCIAL MEDIA and NETWORKING. As I mentioned in my introduction, I created one 12 years ago for my Kenai Central High School Alumni in Alaska.

o The intention was to help reconnect with classmates

and to also be apprised of events or activities related to our Alumni from the 1970's and late 1960's. A type of Community posting Board.

o My GROUP is "KCHS Alumni & CLASSMATES – Kenai Central High School – 1970's, Late 1960's".

- Private Link: https://www.facebook.com/groups/KCHS1970s/.

o To be honest, I created the GROUP because I had missed several event opportunities because I heard about them too late to participate.

- One was an exciting Trip to Europe with the Alumni Choir Trip to sing in Cathedrals! After I missed that event, I became determined to help our group of classmates stay connected.

o The KCHS startup began as a Public GROUP, but eventually became a Private GROUP with parameters for Membership.

- This was also a safeguard to eliminate spammers and non-connected people.

o Recently, our KCHS Class of 1973 celebrated its 50th Class Reunion and used the GROUP to get the word out.

- In September 2022, I started NETWORKING for the Class Reunion by posting on the KCHS Alumni GROUP and inquiring whether my classmates had an interest in attending.

- Once there was a buzz and classmates & friends started responding, I realized Facebook NETWORKING would be one effective way to reach people. Just think, 50 years have passed with no or little connection with most of our classmates!

- Because we have over six hundred members in the KCHS Private GROUP, we were able to create interest in our event more quickly than old-fashioned calling or email.

- As Committee Chair of the Reunion Committee, I recruited a Committee and Volunteer team to create a successful and beautiful outdoor event at Lakeside Falls in Soldotna, Alaska on July 9, 2023.

  - Online ZOOM meetings were used effectively for planning.

- I created a "SAVE-THE-DATE" - RSVP EVENT to obtain preliminary interest and headcount.

  - Invitations were sent out, the EVENT was posted to the KCHS site, and people began responding with "GOING, MAYBE, or NOT GOING."

- During the 10-month period of planning, I created many marketing flyers and material used in EVENTS to spread the word both electronically, and by word-of-mouth. They helped gain attention to our Reunion.

o NOTE: My Facebook Alumni High School GROUP was the first of its kind in the Kenai/Soldotna, Alaska area. It prompted Alumni to form other community Facebook GROUPS as well.

- One is called "A Work in Progress: Growing Up on the Kenai."

- Its purpose is for sharing stories and memories of growing up on the Kenai Peninsula in Alaska, the "last frontier," during the 1950's, 1960's, 1970's.

  - Since its inception, it has had over 5,000 members and the creation of a second GROUP was necessary.

  - It is exciting to know that a book is being created and published with all the memories, history, and photos shared by locals growing up on the Kenai Peninsula in Alaska.

  - A non-profit 501 C3 was formed to manage the book production and administration of both GROUP sites.

- I was credited as being at the helm of this GROUP by one of Alumni Board members. I am immensely proud that initiating NETWORKING via SOCIAL MEDIA 12 years ago prompted this last frontier GROUP.

- A PAGE created on Facebook is an effective way for added NETWORKING and marketing.

  o My first Community Public PAGE was created to share RECIPES entitled "JEANNETTE'S JOY SHARED RECIPES".

    ▪ Public Link: https://www.facebook.com/ JeannettesJoy.

    ▪ It is also the first PAGE I created.

  o Because my Private GROUP "RECIPES from Facebook" was a success, I decided to broaden the audience and concept into a Public PAGE.

    ▪ Please look, as you will find all sorts of delicious recipes, including healthy, decadent, holiday, and fun treats for children or young at heart.

    ▪ The Public PAGE is also set up so that members can post their own interesting recipes to share.

  o A Business PAGE is another Facebook feature that I investigated after using the Community Facebook PAGE.

    ▪ The choice is quite effective and acts as a mini website, blog, newsfeed, and events calendar all-in-one.

- NOTE: The Community PAGE I created and managed for RECIPES had less visibility. This afforded a learning experience for me for future Business PAGES.

o "DJ's Virtual Management/Senior Tech Tutor" is my first Business PAGE.

  - Public Link: https://www.facebook.com/ djsvirtualmanagement.

  - It includes summary information about my business, address, hours, mission, focus, informative articles, training EVENTS, and business services.

  - Most EVENTS are also shared on my personal business website and INSTAGRAM for fuller marketing coverage.

  - This Facebook Business PAGE has also added visibility and effectiveness to my business website.

    - Public Link: https://djsvirtualmanagement. com.

o "JEANNETTE'S JOY" is the second Business PAGE I created when I revamped my entrepreneurial business while also changing the focus and branding.

  - Because of my experience creating the first Business PAGE, the second one was much easier to create, launch and manage.

- JEANNETTE'S JOY introduces my brand, focus, motto, quotes, and additional information.

    - Public Link: https://www.facebook.com/jeannettesjoy88.

- Also effective was the ability to create Facebook EVENTS that are linked directly to my business PAGE.

- My new e-commerce site is also linked to this Facebook PAGE.

    - Public Link: https://thewmarketplace.com/collections/jeannette-s-joy.

- EVENTS feature in Facebook is also an effective option for business or personal activities.

    o When setting up an event on Facebook, basic information is needed, such as location, price, audience, etc. Once set up, the EVENT can be shared on your personal profile, on your business pages, or sent out as an invitation.

    o I recently used the feature with the KCHS Alumni group that I created.

        - I added an EVENT for the planning of our 50th Class Reunion.

        - It was added as both a Post and Invitation with the KCHS Alumni GROUP.

- The SAVE-THE-DATE Invitation prompted classmates to respond with GOING, MAYBE or NOT GOING. This helped in obtaining a preliminary headcount of interested classmates.

- Details of our Facebook EVENT activity are written under the GROUP section.

- Classmates who did not use online Social Media or were not tech savvy were given the information by family or friends who heard about the EVENT on Facebook, local radio station, local newspapers, word-of-mouth sharing, and on the EVENTBRITE website.

EVENTBRITE is an online website used to promote, market, advertise, and purchase advanced tickets to an EVENT.

- Because EVENTBRITE is an online e-commerce type of website, TICKETS to events are advertised and purchased in advance.

- Current Contact Information is also collected from the ticket purchasers.

- The website system also provides various Reports, including Attendee List with detail and various Sales reports. The reports make Attendee tracking and Sales progress much simpler.

- The EVENTBRITE link can also be posted and shared on other SOCIAL MEDIA sites or on invitations.

- My online account was originally set up for my business "DJ's Virtual Management/Senior Tech Tutor."

- I used EVENBRITE to promote my Senior Tech Training Workshops.

  o Pre purchased tickets worked out great for these trainings and gave me a headcount in advance.

- Recently, I used my EVENTBRITE account for our High School 50th Reunion to promote and advertise it.

  o We were able to introduce the location (a new Venue for the geographical area) for the Reunion by adding photos, information, and venue link.

  o The Reunion Date posting on EVENTBRITE helped to obtain a stronger interest in the Reunion.

INSTAGRAM is versatile and easy to use for increasing marketing and networking.

- It is a free Social Media site, which can be linked to other apps such as Facebook and Twitter.

- Many people prefer to have simpler, quicker ways to use Social Media Networking with these more visual websites.

- Sharing my Facebook business posts to INSTAGRAM, or my personal Facebook PROFILE post only requires a few extra keystrokes with little effort!

- Posting on INSTAGRAM increased my audience as they became aware of my other Social Media sites on Facebook, Twitter or to my business website.

GRAPHICS for SOCIAL MEDIA

- Using free apps, such as CANVA and PicCollage, has been fun and dramatically effective in some situations.

- It has been a fun and creative outlet for me and have made graphics, flyers, posters, logos, business cards, invitations, and other graphic documents.

  o I have found ways to engage my audience and grab their attention more often while having fun creating new items.

- It is also easy to post various graphics on Facebook personal or business profiles, PAGES, GROUPS, and EVENTS.

- My flyers and marketing material have helped my SOCIAL MEDIA presence.

BLOG Social Media became an interest of mine about 13 years ago.

- There are many platforms for BLOGS.

  o I chose an easy BLOG format called BLOGSPOT within the free Google apps platform.

- During my research phase, I learned there were several

ways to use a BLOG.

- o One way was posting (like a newspaper feed).

- o Another is a way to monetize a BLOG to make money (with paid advertisers).

- I found interesting BLOG sites that I enjoyed following.

  - o This also helped me to define what I wanted my BLOG to look like and what content I would include.

- My BLOG is entitled "JEANNETTE'S JOY" and was created in November 2010 with a leap of faith.

  - o Public Link: https://jeannettesjoy.blogspot.com.

  - o The creation purpose was not to earn income from advertising, but rather to explore my ability to be an author and figure out if I had an interested audience.

  - o It allowed me to be creative and I was able to establish what became my future BRAND – "JEANNETTE'S JOY" (with PINK colors of course!).

  - o Another motivation was to try out effective writing and decide whether I had enough talent to be a published author of future books and published articles.

  - o My BLOG became a type of Journal or Newsletter, written with certain themes and topics from my heart.

- I have been able to share topics such as: (a) "The Golden Rule" - treating others in a good way that I also want to be treated; (b) Emotional Self-Regulation; (c) Sharing Love with Others; (d) Speaking positiveness in others while they are living; (e) My Life Tribute; (f) Forgiveness - Is it Worth It?; (g) Safe and Secure; and many more topics.

- In my articles, I also add graphics which emphasize the theme – especially for those who are more visual.

- Using researched material, I have also been able to make the articles more interesting.

- Links to YouTube music videos or other news material are also included to gain more interest.

- It has been lovely to share from my heart and I am grateful for the positive feedback received over the years.

- I am still authoring articles or posting graphics which I pray make a positive impact on people's lives.

- As "Jeannette LeHoullier – Joyful Diva," I am compiling many of my BLOG articles for my upcoming book "Life Perspectives by the Joyful Diva."

- An additional book I will publish is entitled "JOYFUL DISCOMBOBULATION" – How to be happy amidst chaos. It will be full of antidotes, humor, and thought-provoking ideas.

LinkedIn is a business-related online platform for BUSINESS networking. The app is designed to network within the business world and add business contacts.

- Everyone creates a type of online resume with more features added.

  o My Public Link is: https://www.linkedin.com/in/jeannettelehoullier

- Its format includes each person's business, work history, work skills, related websites, and employment related posts.

- Many members have found it quite effective for networking with current or past co-workers, related co-workers, employers, future employers, university affiliation, association affiliation, and referrals.

- I have found this to be effective in the business world by reconnecting, networking, and becoming more visible in the work force both as an individual and for business.

- It can be an effective way to promote one's business and for prospective employment staffing.

- I also find posted Articles quite engaging and have shared some to my profile.

- It is also a way to promote oneself with positive feedback from clients or co-workers.

SOCIAL MEDIA NETWORKING can be used in our daily lives and provide additional knowledge on issues of interest to us.

- For instance, I author articles for the Menifee Buzz newspaper using NETWORKING as it relates to Senior Technology and Family Caregiving.

  o Public Link: www.menifeebuzz.com/...family-caregivers...technology. (see below)

Thursday, 06 February 2020

Family Caregivers Using Technology

Save

FAMILY CAREGIVERS UNITE! Help conquer various issues like: Isolation, Boredom, Entertainment as well as practical things like Safety, Organization, Communication, Creativity, Education, Information and Resources.

When we think about being a caregiver, we don't always think about the technological resources available to help us. Dedication, compassion, and time given as a caregiver can be enhanced utilizing technology. As a caregiver, it helps to find ways to make our lives happier and easier.

Isolation, Boredom, Entertainment:

CONNECTION & COMMUNICATION

EXAMPLE: Isolation is deterred when we can see someone "face-to-face" with programs such as Facetime, Skype, and Zoom. For me, there is nothing more precious than chatting with my grandson. What's even better is seeing my grandson via a real time viewing app! It's great to show each other our projects, surroundings, or interaction with pets – a type of "show and tell".

SOLUTIONS: Social Media; Facebook; YouTube; Pinterest; Email; Music; Chat or viewing programs such as Facetime, Skype, and Zoom.

ENTERTAINMENT

EXAMPLE: My 90-year-old Aunt enjoys listening to old time music, like hymns, while watching videos on YouTube. Oftentimes, she is unable to hear or see the screen adequately from my tablet or smartphone. My solution is to project (stream) the video to my smart TV and turn up the volume. Our "smart" technical devices make it quite easy to enjoy this option. This happens easily with just a few clicks.

SOLUTIONS: YouTube, Pandora, iTunes; Websites; Facebook; Games; Streaming to a Smart TV, phone, tablet, or laptop (songs, videos, photos, etc.)

CREATIVITY

EXAMPLE: I enjoy creating cards, flyers, announcements, and ads with photos. There are many options to explore, whether it is for doodling, coloring, or other artistic endeavors.

SOLUTIONS: Pinterest; Photo/Video apps; Drawing/

Coloring; Craft Ideas; APPS: PicCollage or Canva

EDUCATION

EXAMPLE: I've used several online sites to find videos and articles for cooking, hairstyling, business, etc. for just about anything I want to learn.

SOLUTIONS: YouTube; APPS; Pinterest; University and other institutions; Research elder games; Learn "how to" for hobbies, crafts, interests, repairs.

Practical Uses:

SAFETY

EXAMPLE: GPS tracking – I've been using the free app Life360. My aunt's impairment prohibits her from easily contacting me, especially in case of an emergency. The app tracks her GPS physical location throughout the day and provides travel times, distance and even speed of the vehicle she travels in. This helps alleviate anxiety I may feel when my aunt travels without me to adult daycare or spends time outside our home with her contracted caregivers. Security cameras can also be checked from your devices. You can view your loved one while you're away. Navigation apps - Not only can a user find the directions, and be prompted with notifications while driving, it can also inform you of traffic situations that may delay your trip.

SOLUTIONS: GPS tracking (Life360, etc.); Smartwatches

with Voice Connection; Alarm Necklaces; GPS insoles; Safety Cameras (accessible via devices); Alarm systems; Navigation apps (Google Maps, etc.)

ORGANIZATION

EXAMPLE: It is necessary for me to track both my personal and business appointments as well as all activities for my aunt. I use Calendar functions and set Alarms to remind me in advance.

SOLUTIONS: Smartphone or Tablet Calendar; Apps; Outlook (multi functions with calendar, email, and contacts); Document scanning (business cards, physician reports); Contact Lists; Time Management; Communication (Facetiming, Skype); Business tools.

RESOURCES

EXAMPLE:

Network of Care Riverside, Aging and Disabilities - https://riverside.networkofcare.org/aging/

This is an online website Riverside County publishes that offers various solution-oriented options. The site includes a personalized profile, which can be shared with other family members or caregivers. It is a type of diary or online entry system to keep track of meds, doctor's appointments, lab tests, or other pertinent information helpful to a person's care needs. There is also an option to print a medical card with information you provide into the secured profile of the website.

SOLUTIONS: Internet; Networking; Tools (calculator, compass, flashlight); Alexa; Siri; Website: Network of Care of Riverside for Aging and Disability

INFORMATION

EXAMPLE: Online Medical Portals are common with many physician offices. It provides access to medical records, health summaries, lab test results, and other medical related information. Records can be downloaded and printed for your files, or in advance of seeing a secondary physician, or specialist. My aunt was able to use this prior to seeing a new specialist and expedite receiving her medical information, eliminating contact directly with her primary doctor's office.

SOLUTIONS: Internet; Apps; Websites; YouTube; Sales and Purchasing (Etsy, Amazon, eBay, Stores, etc.; Siri or Google; Physician medical portal.

Don't let caregiving limit you without resources. Enhance your life with technology. Try out one of these options and see if it makes a difference in your life.

To contact Jeannette LeHoullier at DJ's Virtual Management, call her at 951-595-7248 (cell). Access her website for additional information and tutoring options www.djsvirtualmanagement.com. Their motto: "Assist with Integrity, Compassion and Patience."

NETWORKING IS SO WORTHWHILE!!   Especially

when it helps others further their own Social Media Networking.

In closing, I hope you have realized there are multiple ways to use NETWORKING with SOCIAL MEDIA in both your Personal and Business endeavors. Remember this: You decide what is comfortable, safe, and efficient for your standards and interests. There is no one set rule in using technology to increase your connections. Explore and see what works best for you. Wishing you many blessings on your day.

QUESTIONS FOR CONSIDERATION:

How many platforms are you using to expose your content?

How many business pages are you posting on, and what platforms are you using?

Are these pages helping me to expand my business?

Dr. Sara M. Lypps (h.c.), MBA

The True Power of Effective Networking

Have you ever wondered if all of the networking you've been doing over the years is really paying off? Now, this is a fully loaded question, and for good reason. First, let me say that I completely believe in the power and potential of networking and more so, in "Effective Networking." No one ever taught me the true power and true potential of networking when it's performed the right way. This technique is something that I had to learn on my own after several decades of trial and error. Second, most people think, or they've been led to believe, that networking is an opportunity to immediately grow their business and do something to add to their bottom line. This might be the case in certain circumstances for a few entrepreneurs, but for the majority of us, networking is not a quick fix to enhance our revenue significantly over lunch or happy hour. In addition, networking is not something that should be viewed on a transactional level. You may go to an event and host a table to sell your services, and even make a few bucks, but at the end of the day, it's not about what you sell or what you do, it's about who you are and how you show up to support others while building relationships.

In this chapter, I hope to not only help you gain some valuable perspective on the importance of "Effective Networking," but also to entertain you with some fun and powerful stories relating to this critical topic. Just so you know, networking can take on many different appearances. Networking is happening in and through you in several different types of social situations, it just may not be labeled as such. I have met some of my best clients in the grocery store by merely having a conversation about life and being concerned about their well-being. It can certainly take longer for these relationships to mature, but it is well worth the effort, for these are very unique and special indeed.

So, in actuality, how many different ways can we network for our business or promote our products? There are too many ways to mention in just one chapter, but let's discuss a few. One of the most popular ways to network is to attend a live networking event. Depending on your profession, this could take place at any number of groups and locations. At first, it can be quite overwhelming to research and determine what group is the best fit for you. Usually, the best place to start is one where you are invited by a friend or acquaintance. This way, you have a wing man, or wing woman, so to speak, that is looking out for you and can offer you a warm introduction to other networkers. If you're in a group of 20-30 or more, it's very unlikely that you will have an opportunity to get to meet and talk with everyone in the room. However, if you have an "in" with someone who has been to that meeting before, or is possibly running the meeting, it is not improper for you to ask to be introduced to a few people. Now, you don't want to just talk to anyone, at least initially, but rather ask to meet the top three most influential people in the room. Even if these few people don't necessarily need your goods or services, they are more likely to know someone in the room or within the community that does. These people are called, "connectors!" They are special for several reasons. First, they are always looking for ways to be of service. Although you might think that you are burdening them by asking for their time, they have been called to a higher mission. They love to connect with like-minded people that are able to work together for a common cause. Second, they may have people they know that have been looking to connect with someone who does what you do; you will never know that unless you ask to start a conversation. So don't be shy! And finally, be open to unexpected opportunities. Networking is not just about finding ways to make money; it's about seeking ways to help others in business. Maybe you meet someone who has an event coming up in a few weeks that still needs a few volunteers to get things to run smoothly. It's an extremely nice gesture to offer help, even on a low commitment, and in return you might even get some support on your project when you need it. Regardless, you are telling the universe that you are open to being of service and the "Law of Attraction" will be sounded to hopefully bless you soon in return.

Now, I'd like to share a little story about a very structured networking group that I attended a few years ago. This networking group that I am referring to had a very expensive cost of entry, and an even higher commitment level. This group met every week at the same time at a restaurant for lunch that was extremely overpriced and at a location that took me nearly an hour to get to. However, after I paid the $400 membership fee to join, I personally and professionally agreed to myself to make a solid commitment to stick it out for the current year. And so, I did! Week after week, I would drop my two young boys off at school, get ready and put my game face on, and drive an hour to meet people that I thought could help me grow my business. Although we did have a few guests come, or potential new members, for the most part, it was just the same, 15-20 people week after week after week. Now, did I mention that being a member of this chapter we were required to offer referrals as a part of the networking group? In the 52 weeks that I was part of this group, never did one qualified referral come through to me. As a Comprehensive Financial Advisor, I was looking to team up with: An Estate Planning Attorney, Real Estate Agent, Loan Officer, Property and Casualty Insurance Agent, Divorce Attorney, etc. ALL OF THE PEOPLE ON MY WISH LIST WERE IN THE ROOM! However, the mentality still remained to be, "How can you help me?" and NOT, "How can I help you?" This forever changed how I looked at so called, "Networking Events." Although this networking group was nearly a professional and financial disaster, something very unexpected came out of it. I will gladly share that with you a little later in the story; it'll be worth the wait!

So, if structured networking isn't always beneficial, what about random networking? It truly depends on the definition of "random." There are always opportunities that come up to network at new and possibly undisclosed locations. However, it's a good idea to know ahead of time what the group's mission or theme of the group is ahead of time. I've been to political groups, religious groups, community service groups, business groups, etc. and most of which have their own agenda which doesn't necessarily mean helping to support you and your goal as an entrepreneur. Know the background and hidden agenda of your group before you attend. Show up, be your authentic and best self, have a heart to serve, and know that business opportunities are available all around you if you just pay attention to the people and work on building lasting relationships. The potential for success isn't just because you're at a so-called networking event, it's because you're putting your best foot forward to truly make a difference in your community.

Another topic I'd like to cover, I'm going to call, "Over Networking." Have you ever been to so many networking events in a week that you couldn't even see straight? I've been there firsthand! Initially, it seems like fun and the possibilities for success are infinite, but then reality sets in. How can you possibly talk to and connect to everyone in the room? The answer is, "You can't!" For most typical networking events, you have an hour and a half to two hours to place your order and get your food, eat, and then mingle. This can be very challenging depending on the venue. Now, I've had weeks where I went to 3-4 networking events and, although I enjoyed myself, I truly didn't feel like I made any real connections. Maybe it was because I felt rushed to eat and then settled in before the speaker began. Or perhaps, I had several shallow, but perceived as meaningful conversations with fellow guests, that ended up nowhere. I would leave networking events with dozens of business cards, but I was lost as to where to go next to reach out to them. Do you put their business card in a shoe box, put them on a mailing list, call them and leave a message, send an email or a text? While there is no one right answer, the first two responses are not options. You must take action after you meet someone at a networking event, but aggressive action is not productive nor appreciated without the other parties' consent. Rather then, when you meet someone for the first time, ask them what their preferred method of conversation is. YOU WILL MOST LIKELY NEVER GET THE SAME ANSWER! Some people are old school and only like to communicate via telephone. Others are very visual and prefer to have all of their correspondence sent via email. While the rest like communication up close and personal and prefer text messages. You won't know for sure unless you spend the time to get to know them and their unique networking love language.

Just a fun fact, some of my biggest clients didn't come from a networking event, but some of my best friends did. You never know who you are going to meet unless you, "suit up, show up," and what I like to call "shut up." The best way to connect with others is to ask sincere questions and be a good listener. You are not there to blah blah blah about you and what you need. Share genuine concern for others and show them that you have a heart to serve; the relationships will magically happen when you do. Financial success and abundance are inevitable when you are honest and real. Most often people think that networking is a one-way street, but it is truly when you give to others in this setting that you will receive something unexpected. Maybe a new client, an opportunity for a joint venture, or even better, a new friend can come out of you showing up and being an authentic you.

One of my favorite things to do in a social setting is to share knowledge by educating, empowering, and encouraging others. This can be an extremely powerful tool when done correctly. Networking events can be a great opportunity to speak. Now I'm not talking about just a thirty second or a one-minute elevator pitch, but an actual opportunity to speak and get out your message to the community in a bigger way. Speaking in front of networking groups, or any group for that matter, is an amazing time to be able to connect with your audience and make an impact. My rule of thumb is whether you're speaking to a group of tens or hundreds of people, just impact the life of one person. Of course, there are very likely many more that will be positively affected by your message, but you only need one person to be changed forever to make a huge difference in this world. Stop and take a few breaths to really let that sink in. "Change a Life, Change the World!"

So, what is "Effective Networking?" It's really whatever truly works for you. Every networker has different needs, different opportunities, and different skill sets. However, we all have the same 24 hours in a day to eat, sleep, practice good self-care, take care of our family, (fur family included), and run our businesses. So, let's not waste our time doing activities that aren't serving us and helping us grow professionally and personally. What do I actually mean by that? Do what feels good! If you're part of a networking group that makes you wonder about who you are, maybe it's time to move on. Life's too short to allow others to question your integrity or your intentions. "Just be you!" Also, if you really like to volunteer, then do more of that and enjoy doing it. You will meet the right people no matter what the environment you're in when you feel appreciated and are being your true and authentic self, doing what you love.

So where are the best places to network? Again, there are too many to list but a great place to start is to go with a friend or acquaintance that has been to a particular group before and come as their guest. Not every group is going to be a perfect fit, but you're getting out there and meeting new people and you never know what doors may open for you. An amazing mentor and friend of mine, Sharon Lechter often says, "One phone call can change your life!" This doesn't mean that you should be sitting on your phone at home like you're about to hatch an Easter egg, but rather that by going out in the world and meeting new people, you never know who you're going to meet. All it takes is one significant connection to positively change your life forever, but you have to be open to the experience and enjoy the journey.

Remember back to my story of being extremely frustrated with dead end and hopeless weekly networking groups? The silver lining is I met one of my nearest and dearest friends in that group; it was completely unexpected. If I had given up after only a few months, I would have missed out on the opportunity to meet someone who not only inspires me but also laughs at all of my jokes. Our friendship has been as amazing blessing years later, on so many levels. My point is, be prepared to be pleasantly surprised. Even if one group isn't a good fit for you, you just might meet someone who helps open a door to one, that is. So, show up in order to see the possibilities in the next chapter of your life. You never know who you might meet that could change your life and catapult you where you want to go. Moreover, the real blessing is, you never know whose life you could positively affect and make a real difference that could change them in their trajectory. In closing, remember to be approachable, be mindful, be intentional, be a good listener, and most of, be kind.

QUESTIONS FOR CONSIDERATION:

How do I show up to support others?

Can I describe myself as a Connector?

How many ways can I network for my business? What can I share?

What do with business cards after a meeting?

Do I have a system where I can easily retrieve information for following up?

Where are the best places to network?

What is a good strategy to use when I am trying to build relationships?

Dr. Susie Mierzwik (h.c.)

Networking With Intention

As with so many other things in life, when it comes to Networking, it is "All in Your Head." What I mean is that all the outcomes of networking come from Intention. My intention is to get to know new people within the group each time I am present. Although I DO greet the members who I already know, I spend the greatest portion of my time approaching those I haven't met. When I spot someone, I don't know yet, sitting or standing alone, I immediately go over to them to introduce myself, and welcome them to the function. I spend several minutes finding out about them. When I see another member of the group, I engage that person and introduce the first timer to my colleague. In this way, the new person has someone else to speak with, as I make my way around the room. I don't drop that person and leave them alone.

Intention means everything in networking, and I use a

discipline whenever I do it, either in person or in a virtual group. In every case, I chose at least three people in the group with whom I plan to do some follow-up.

I always make a brief note about each new acquaintance, either on their card, or in my own calendar. I write down where we met and a key item to jog my memory about our conversation. Where discipline comes into play is with my follow-up. Usually within 2 days of our meeting, I reach out to my new acquaintances by text or email. I ask if they would like to zoom together to further our connection. This strategy does not always result in a new customer, but it does ensure that the next time we meet, we are no longer strangers. When we see each other again, now I can ask about their business, family, or special interest, because we have established a basis of conversation.

Since I want my new acquaintances to feel connected, I often invite the newbies to another mutually beneficial networking group. When getting to know someone, I ask many questions about them. I don't talk much about myself, except on areas we share in common. I use these commonalities to strengthen our connection. Most people talk willingly about themselves and will feel that I am interested in them. Usually when they have talked freely for a while, they will then ask about me. If my new acquaintance has a product available for purchase, sometimes I buy it. I always talk about their business before I mention my own.

Networking is a way of life for me. If I discover that my new friend has a store I can patronize or a book I can purchase,

I may do that, because it increases the likelihood of staying connected in the future. This gives me more information about the new person, so I can discover if there is a way, I can serve them.

It takes discipline to remember to follow up with new people. I use my daily calendar and also my daily planner to make notes of phone calls, emails, or texts I need to make each day. If I get no answer, then I can add that name to another date on the calendar.

What about established clients? I have created the discipline of connecting with my current clients on a regular basis with either a text, phone call or email. Sometimes I will send the link to a You- Tube video they may find interesting or informative. I will keep in touch with sales specials and webinars they can attend. I always include a personal note reminding them I am always available for questions or consultations.

If I promise to send someone information, I always follow up. It takes discipline but my promises are never idle. That's a fact.

Another tool I maintain is a notebook. I write down the name of the meeting, group, or webinar where I met a new contact. I will write a detail that stands out to me, whether it is a health issue they are concerned about or a mutual acquaintance. For example, "Mary Smith, GSFE group, concerned about blood sugar/ knows Robbie Motter." It is important to write down where I met the new contact. When I am connected to many people in my life, I want to remember how I found each one individually. I show people that meeting them was important enough to me and that I remember how we met.

Another tool that is vital in networking is using a name tag. I want people to know my name and not feel embarrassed wondering who I am. As soon as I meet a new person, I use their name in the conversation immediately. If I forget, I ask again, I'm sorry, what is your name again? I never leave the conversation unless I am sure of their name. No guessing allowed. How can I follow up if I am not even sure who I was speaking to?

When I meet new people, I make it a point to find a common bond. It could be anything, from a mutual acquaintance, their profession or where they are from. If I discover someone from a place I've never been, then I ask many questions about their area. If we have professional interests in common, then I explore that avenue in the conversation.

If I detect an accent in my new acquaintance, I ask about their background or travel experience. Most people feel comfortable talking about themselves. There are many avenues to pursue regarding travel, either I have been there, or I know little about their area, and I have lots of questions to ask them about their country, state, or city. After I find out something about their life, I may broach the topic of my business as it pertains to them. But the majority of the conversation is centered on them, never me.

The discipline of networking is a way of life I carry out daily. This happens wherever I travel as well as in my local area. When I was on safari in Africa, I discovered that the owner of one of the lodges we stayed at was suffering from back pain. I made it a point to seek her out and connect. I took away her back pain and gained a new international client.

At another networking event, I discovered that one of the entertainers was an Olympic athlete. When I followed up with her, I introduced her to the Olympic athlete connection with Lifewave; this is the nondrug pain relief that is used by Olympic athletes in my business. This interaction resulted in getting new business in Canada, the United States, and the Philippines.

If I meet someone who speaks another language, I will try to say something in their native language, even if it is just Hello or thank you or goodbye. It shows respect for others when we say something in their native tongue.

On an airplane recently, I heard the flight attendant speaking in Spanish. I used my elementary skills to chat in Spanish. She was surprised, but I told her I enjoyed having the opportunity to practice. Another time, the fellow travelers at our table were speaking French. Again, I used my basic knowledge of French to get to know them a little bit.

Afterwards, I might ask the person if they would like to get more information about Lifewave, since my business is international. If they say yes, then I have acquired another international client.

Besides speaking to a person in their native language a bit, another way I like to deepen the connection is by discovering who else we may know in common. I notice that this technique is an effective way to build rapport with someone I have just met. If we both have common acquaintances, this warms up the conversation considerably and increases the trust factor. It is a good principle to get to know someone first before approaching them about business. In the first contact, I usually stick with nonbusiness related conversation. No one wants to feel they are just being targeted for a sale. We all know that people do business only with those they know, like and trust. So, if this goal is not accomplished first, there will never be any business later on.

Genuine interest in learning about people is a basic tool needed when networking. I make it a practice to carry on a conversation with everyone. In a cab recently, I inquired where the driver was from. When he said Turkey, I asked about the recent earthquake and if his family was safe. Another time I noticed the driver wore a special kind of necklace. I asked him if he was a Coptic Christian? An amazing smile appeared on his face when he told me he was from Egypt.

A good opening question in making a new acquaintance is asking how long someone has lived in their current area. This creates many avenues of conversation about their homeland, history, family, career and so much more. I ask open-ended questions so the person can respond in any way they like. I can tell by the enthusiasm in their answers if they want to pursue the conversation.

In short, having a sincere love of people is the best discipline to use in networking throughout your life. If we want to connect with people, wherever we meet them, we will have a never-ending stream of contacts, clients, and friends.

QUESTIONS FOR CONSIDERATION:

When I go to an event do still feel comfortable to sit with only the people I know?

Why is my intention during this event?

How do I perceive a new person?

Do I make them feel welcome?

How will I start a conversation to get to know them?

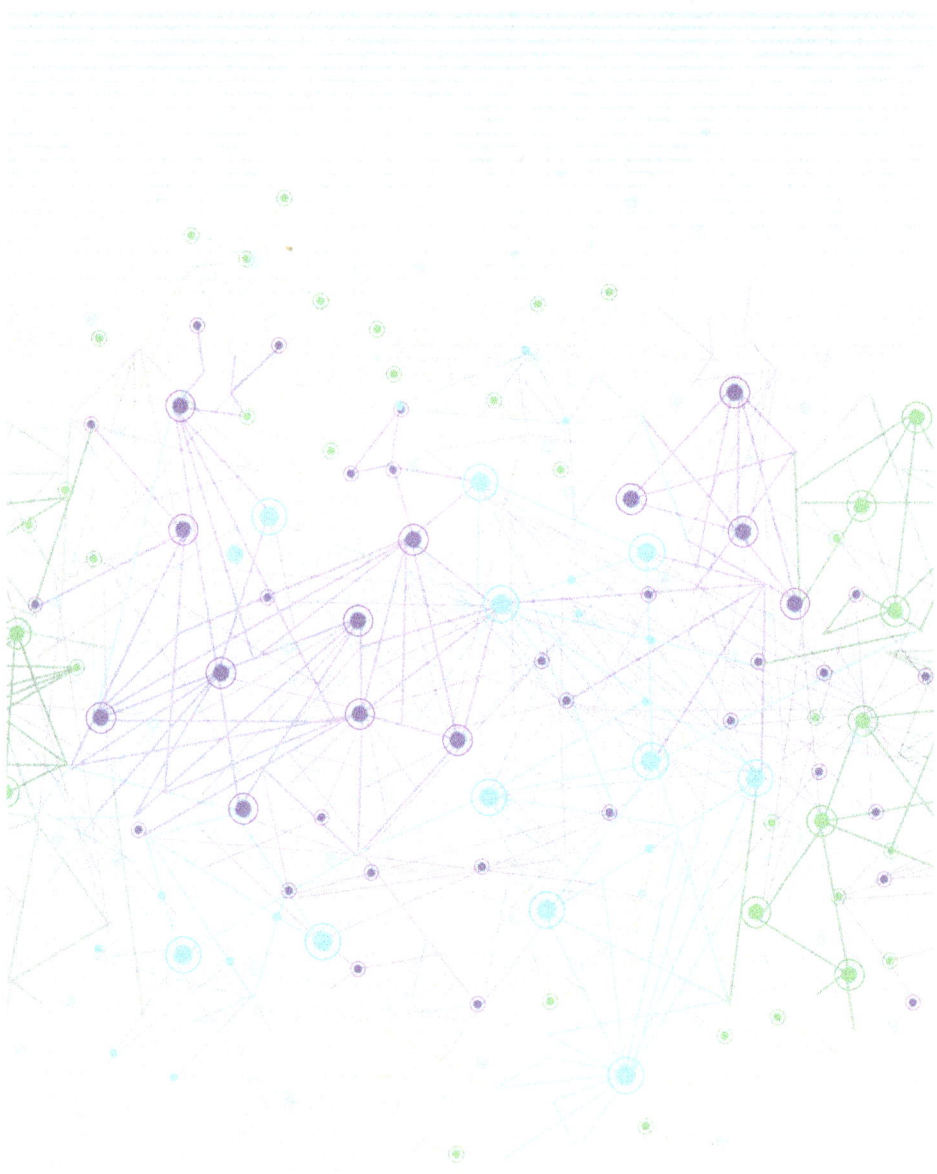

Dr. Ramin Modiri, (h.c.)

It's Not All About Your IQ

Appointed as Chair of Education for one of the most prominent Investment Foundation for 11 years, the most common question was how to obtain the ideal job and become wealthy. My answer, to this day, is that the most important wealth is not the financial one but rather the network of people that you know.

To accumulate this wealth, Academia and our education system highlights the IQ and academic achievement above all else. This might be true when it comes to a specialized field such as quantum physics and medicine, I believe there are many other attributes to one's success.

With the emergence of Artificial intelligence and Chat GPT, this is more evident than ever. For the first time it is innovative and executive positions are at the risk of elimination rather than more of the manufacturing and service jobs that had been replaced by technological improvements. (Think of Robotics and factory workers or 450,000 Telephone operators in the 1950s or millions of typists in the 1970s.)

The idea is that there should be more emphasis on EQ which is your Emotional Quotient and Social Quotient than just the Intellectual Quotient. As a matter of fact, according to Howard Gardner's theory of multiple intelligences there are 7 types of Intelligence that are present...

1. Linguistic (reading, writing, speaking, and listening,)

2. Logical-Mathematical (reasoning, problem-solving, logical, mathematical abilities)

3. Musical (understanding patterns, tones, and rhythms.)

4. Spatial (three-dimensional view of things, visual thinking)

5. Kinesthetic and Physical (coordination, body control)

6. Interpersonal (understanding others, empathy, communication, social awareness.)

7. Intrapersonal (self-awareness, self-reflection.)

In order to build relationships for wealth through networking I share my 7 principles and strategies:

1- Be Clear about Your Goals And be Purposeful.

Know what you are networking for. Is it for getting clients? Is it for a new Career? Is it building a network for future projects?

2- Have a Niche and be an Expert

In the 1980s every investment advisor was focusing on the US Markets. With my background, I decided to focus on international finance and be the specialist in Emerging Markets, Currencies and Commodities.

3- Be a Good Listener and Humble

In the 1990s I used to attend events At World Affairs Council regularly. At one of the events, I noticed an elderly gentleman sitting by himself at the table. I approached him and asked him if could sit next to him. In turn he replied "of course." He asked me what I did and at that time I was managing portfolios mainly in Emerging Markets. With his interest piqued, he pursued more insight on my career. With the conversation continuing, another elderly gentleman joined us and asked me if I had learned something sitting next to and talking to the founder and CEO of one of the largest investment companies in America.

4- Be Present

One of the highlights of my life was sitting with Pele, perhaps the greatest Soccer player, for 2 hours in an event honoring the Brazilian National team in 1994, the team that eventually won the World Cup that Year. Being so close to Pele, it created an atmosphere so palpable, I became listened to instead of hearing with my ears. His experience and wisdom, especially his challenges to success bridged the gap between my mind and my soul, making me feel enlightened.

5- Provide Services and Value

In the 1980s at the age of 22 I joined the Rotary Club, and I was by far the youngest member. I was there to offer my services and I had many ideas to get more exposure towards the younger generation and fundraising areas. I printed T-Shirts in different languages to reach out to the international communities. My efforts were well noticed and appreciated and even after 20 years I was still being rewarded for my genuine contribution. Remember, you are serving the network and the mission, and not the network and mission serving you.

6- Be Yourself, Authentic and Genuine

Join the Network because you genuinely enjoy being around the group. Offer sincere help and go along for the ride.

7- Be Patient and Always Follow Up

Maintaining relationships is crucial. After meeting someone, stay in touch through a variety of means. Stay engaged and offer relevant information to your group. Remember building r relationships takes time and effort.

Use your social media, ask for help, and seek mentorship.

When it comes to networking for wealth, it is not just about financial gains. Focus on authentic connections and building a genuine relationship. Offer from your heart and be clear on your journey. With patience you will receive many rewards while you are helping your community. Remember connecting is the best way to network.

QUESTIONS FOR CONSIDERATION:

What are your thoughts in real life, should emphasis be more on EQ (Emotional Quotient) and SQ (Social Quotient) than IQ (Intellectual Quotient)?

The author reminds us to be a good listener and be humble. Why?

What is the difference between being a good listener and being present, than anxiously waiting to be heard?

When is it appropriate to ask for help?

What service can you provide for your network?

How reliable are you?

Lady Ambassador Dr. Robbie Motter (h.c.)

Opportunities In Networking,
Thinking Outside The Box

Networking is always in constant change and in today's world it's nothing like it was before. There are so many ways to network but the first thing that has to happen is that you have to get in our head that it has changed, and you need to change our mindset to see the new ideas that are all around us.

People no longer want you to shove a business card in their face, networking today is about building relationships and that takes time, it does not happen overnight. It also means we have to get rid of the ME mentality and go for the WE mentality as WE together can do so much more.

If you're in business, you probably have a business plan and a marketing plan, but do you have a networking plan? That is an important tool as it makes you think about what you hope to accomplish and to do that where is the best place for you to SHOW UP.

Here are some thoughts to think about; you probably have a wad of business cards all over the place that you have collected over time, how about going back to some of those people who you feel are the perfect person to connect with and see how they are, what are they doing now and most importantly is there something you can do to help them. Take time to listen, as there are always so many clues that are given on what their needs might be. If you take time and listen, then you can come back and offer them a solution if it's something you can do or connect them with someone else.

Another think I have observed people go to events to meet people and they sometimes go with friends, so what I have observed is that they hang out with that person the whole time instead of venturing out by themselves so that they can reach out and meet new people. The people you know you can always connect with, so plan to meet so many people everywhere you go. Key is to also follow up with them so much is lost in not following up.

If you have a networking plan you can set steps like I will show up live at so many places a week, I will show up online so many times a week, my goal is to meet x number of new people and to reconnect with x number of people I already know.

Have you ever thought who is your best customer? Where do they show up at? Are they sending you referrals? Are you doing anything for them? Those are all questions you should be looking at as to get you also need to give.

When doing social media are you just clicking like and not even reading the postings? You are missing so many opportunities as every day on social media there are so many opportunities.

I want you to think about this, you're on social media and someone is posting that they are speaking at an event. If you're a speaker yourself what does that tell you? Well as a speaker what it tells me is that where this person is speaking brings in speakers, and I know I cannot speak there this year if they are already totally booked but I could get the contact person and get my name in for their next event they bring in speakers. I personally have done that and shared that with members who did get in to speak and never thought about it as an opportunity.

Did you know that being on a talk show on TV or a RADIO Show is another form of Networking? Yes, it is as each show you are on has a different audience and every time you are a guest you get to meet new people and they get to meet you. So, you're on social media and someone posts I am going to be a guest on this particular show, you should immediately get your pen and paper and write that show name down and contact that show for you to be a guest. Before you do that, have some ideas of the different topics on which you can speak. Here is a source to find places looking for guests as well as for a nominal fee you can post your talent and have them contact you. Podcastguests. com, Most of the hundreds of shows don't charge to be a guest and some do, so you need to look at what show best meets who you are.

Another great way to network is to have a book and do book signings. In today's world you don't need to write that whole book, look for collaborations where you can be a coauthor in a book. This is my preferred way for me, I have been in forty books as a coauthor that means my story is being marketed in many locations, I did write my own book but prefer the collaborations. You can knock one of those stories out in a day and it goes into a book with other amazing stories, and I believe collaborations sell more books, as if they don't like my story, they will like others in the book. So, the book continues to sell. The first collaboration I put together with Authors for GSFE was "It's All About SHOWING UP and the POWER is in the ASKING. That book was published Dec 2022 with forty-six coauthors, and it is still selling today. March 8, 2023, I put together another collaboration with 64 Co-authors, the book title is the same one we added Volume 2 on the cover. Both books made #1 US and International day 1 and 2 after the launch.

Everyone has a story in them and if you have not written a book or been part of a book you need to do that now as that is a big tool for networking.

One of my members two years ago told me she could not write I told her that is just an excuse, you can talk it into your phone and have someone type it out or get ghost writer and that her story for her legacy needed to be told. So, she recorded it in her phone, got someone to type it and published it and it was a US and International Best seller, so what is your excuse?

Staying in touch with me is another valuable networking tool. I use Birthdaycards.com and when GSFE gets new members I add all their birthdays to this program, and it automatically notifies me when it's their birthday and I select a card from their big array of cards to send to them and add my comments as well. I also use Llerrah.com they have fabulous online Cards for all other holidays as they are beautifully done with music. They also have Birthday Cards. Both are very inexpensive every year.

They are not the only ones, there are numerous other sources, this just happens to be the ones I have selected. I always get such nice notes when I send them as sometimes, I just send them just because and it seems that on that day the person getting the card really needed it and it made them happy and so when you do things like this you stay in people's minds and hearts.

I want to get back to the Social Media idea. Through using social media, I met one person from London three years ago, I always commented on her post, it ended up that she invited me to London to stay with her at her home. She then introduced me to some powerful influencers and through them I met others and that is how I now get to nominate my members if deserving for an Honorary Humanitarian Doctorate degree,

I have been invited to London twice that I went and met more people through my contact more opportunities happened. Last year was invited to Thailand and this year have been invited to speak in Johannesburg, South Africa and also through another connection to speak in Chicago, Il.

My last trip to London this year through another person I met in London I was able to take 26 of my GSFE Members while they were there in London for their Honorary Humanitarian Degree we were invited to go to Parliament, receive an award and speak there as well, again through my networking connections we were invited to several other events and this year taking 40 GSFE members to Atlanta o get their Honorary Doctorate Humanitarian degree. All these actions came because I took time to read social media differently, I now ready it only for opportunities. I have been telling my GSFE members to do that as well and one contacted me the other day and say, "Robbie I found 14 opportunities on social media today by reading it for opportunity, it was amazing and it works," she said.

As I said in the beginning the new Networking is about SHOWING UP, ASKING, building relationships, and doing a variety of things, doing TV and Radio SHOWS, writing a Book and so much more, so change your thinking and step out and step up and see the wonderful things that will happen for you in your life.

QUESTIONS FOR CONSIDERATION:

What factors are in the ME mentality?

How can I change my ME Mentality to a WE mentality?

Do I need a networking plan?

Why is it advantageous / not advantageous to hang out with people you know?

How can you creatively get Speakers from Social Media Platforms?

When I Show Up at an Event, am I prepared to network? What resources are available for me that I can provide to the people I interact with?

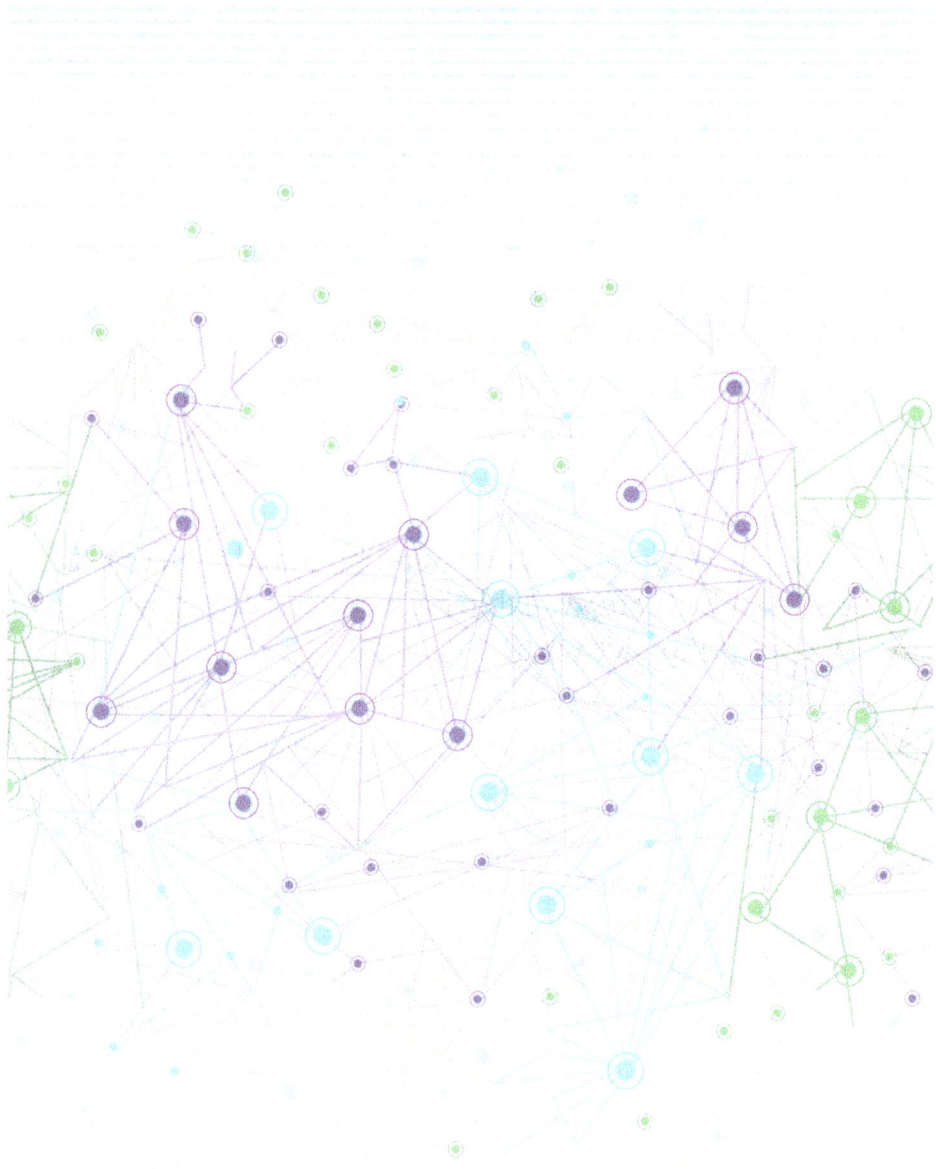

Christine Park

Networking Through The Seasons of Life

Throughout our lives, we are constantly networking and quite often do not realize it. Networking is the process of making connections and building relationships. Effective networking leads to success as we navigate through the seasons of life.

As youths, we make connections and build relationships with family, friends, teachers, and other adults we look up to. This introduction to networking sets the foundation for our future success. This is where we begin to investigate who and what we want to be when we grow up and what we need to do to get there.

As a young child, the domino effect began. I talked loudly, which lead to the realization that I had a hearing problem. Hearing issues lead to speech impairments. Strange and frequent clumsiness lead to the finding of vision problems;

I saw two doorways and would walk through the wrong one. I would write my letters backwards and would read and write right to left. I was taken to several specialists at the time and my young mother was told to put me in a home and leave me there since I would be deaf and dumb, most likely with the intellect of a toddler. My mom did not take his advice and worked with me as best she could and fought to get me the help I would need to navigate through life.

It was later discovered that my hearing difficulties were due to nerve damage caused by a high fever during chicken pox. I unconsciously learned to read lips from the age of two and would lower my voice to what I perceived as a whisper. I focused on learning sounds, even though it could be entertaining from time to time as "tr" came out "f." Some of the vision issues were corrected with glasses although my case was complex which led to more specialists. It was discovered that my brain did not naturally invert the images that I saw. At that time, there was not a lot known about dyslexia. Finally, we are getting somewhere; I am a lefthanded dyslexic. If it were not for networking, I would have been sitting in that home rotting away. My mother and I were networking through the medical sector.

Throughout my school years, I was networking and never knew it. Teachers saw strengths in me I never realized. In academics, teachers would encourage me to try new things and pushed me to do better. This networking led to representing NW Pennsylvania in the Hugh O'Brien Leadership Conference my sophomore year. Even though I was shy and lacked self-confidence, I was active in various groups and activities, networking through the teenage season of life. This networking led to several accomplishments including becoming a member of Who's Who Among American High School Students my junior and senior years. Our childhood aspirations may change frequently as we continue to forge new relationships and grow into the next season of life.

Our journey continues with twists and turns. Sometimes we effectively navigate through the academic world developing connections and relationships through professors, mentors, internships and more. We are adding experiences and steppingstones to acquire the career we desire. At seventeen, I really did not know which way I wanted to proceed. My parents wanted me to go to college, get a degree and embark on a professional career. I utilized basic networking skills applying to and being accepted to Penn State University. During the summer between high school and college I entertained my creative side and constant desire to learn new things. I enrolled at Penn State Cosmetology pursuing a Cosmetology License. I chose the accelerated route with the intention of working as a Cosmologist to aid in financing my college degree. At one point, I was attending both Cosmetology School and Penn State University. I completed cosmetology school, took my state boards, and obtained my Cosmetology License. I quickly secured a position at a salon and began working and meeting people from all walks of life. I continued my Liberal Arts education, majoring in Early Childhood Developmental Psychology. The networking we do during this season of life helps set us up to become successful in our chosen career.

Life has a way of throwing us a curve ball and derails even best made plans. I found myself sliding into the next season of life; married with children. I put my college education on hold with full intentions of continuing later. Parenthood is challenging to say the least, yet networking continues. Playdates for our children, occasional adult conversation for Mom, doctors, teachers, retailers the lists of people and networking opportunities grow. One day, two husbands and four children later, you show up at a PTA meeting and you get sucked into a whole other world. I was the president of the Head Start group where I attended the National Head Start Conference in Washington, DC. Networking on a national level gave me skills and contacts that led me to advocate for early education and especially for children with learning disabilities. Simultaneously, I was the Treasurer of the PTA at the Elementary School where I coordinated the Book Fairs, the fundraising events, as well as advocating for students and parents for several years where, as a parent advocate, I attended the same continuing education and seminars as the teachers. Since all my children were in school now, I became an on-call secretary for the School District as well as an on-call Head Start teacher for the county. Never think, I am just a mom. You are much more than that as once pointed out by an insurance agent. Much to my husband's dismay, I required a heftier life insurance policy than he did. It would cost more to replace what I contributed to the family than the income he contributed. We continue to network without realizing it.

The networking we subconsciously do can lead to limitless possibilities. I now enter the next season in life, as my children follow their educational journey, my husband and I decide to take leap into the business world and self-employment. We started our first uniform shop on a shoestring budget and learned as we went. Who knew all those skills as a mom and networking throughout the years would be so beneficial. Business plans needed to be written, business licenses needed secured, bookkeeping skills needed sharpened, financial, employer and tax reports needed compiled and filed, communication skills needed refined, HR skills needed updated, locations needed secured, leases negotiated, advertising, inventory; the list goes on. Hard work and perseverance and continued networking, in time, led to 3 Uniform and simultaneously, 3 Tuxedo shops, a Tailor shop and finally a Security Company.

Networking plays a large role in business success. Each business and the contacts that were made seamlessly led to subsequent businesses. Decades later, life experiences and networking relationships developed into a teaching position at a Technical Training and Career Center. I taught the Administrative Assistant Program: Accounting 1, Accounting 2, Computerized Accounting, General Office procedures and Basic Computer Skills were among the classes I taught while still operating several businesses. As seasons come to an end so ends the profitability of some businesses. While the choice to close any business is difficult, the knowledge and satisfaction of an unexpected career choice to build a business from the bottom up and raise a family doing so is quite rewarding. The connections that networking award us continues into our next season of life.

As I moved into my next season of life, I find myself divorced, again, and living across the country from where I grew up and raised my family. It was not easy being over fifty and starting over again but I used my unconscious networking abilities as well as all the skills as a business owner, teacher, and mother to find a new vocation in Senior Care. Experiencing all aspects of the trade, I found a Senior Care Networking Group that helped me market the business I worked for and well as market myself. Turnover in the Senior care field is frequent, and you need to keep your options open and professional contacts up to date. I quickly became the Treasurer of this Non-profit Networking Organization. I also took my experience as a business owner and secured additional employment in the Security field. I obtained additional security qualifications and licenses in California, Arizona and Nevada and embarked on new endeavors. This is when I went into working security full time. I had no friends or family in California, so I worked 77 hours a week for one security company and close to 40 hours a week for a second security company. Working security expanded my networking circle to extend into the music, movie, promotional and sports industries.

Once again, seasons changed, and I was reunited with a lost love from my youth, and we began to build a life together. A debilitating work injury left me disabled and spiraling into a complex medical anomaly. We moved twice within southern California finally landing in a quiet 55+ community. I continue to utilize my contacts in Senior Care. I became active in the community and began to make friends. I was introduced to a wonderful networking group, GSFE. Global Society for Female Entrepreneurs is a non-profit organization that helps women network through workshops and events. A group where we do not compete with each other; we complete each other. I found that even though I am no longer a businesswoman, I have a lot of different experiences and a wealth of information that I can share with others.

Life's journey may not be exactly how we intended it to be but through the wonderful process of making connections and building relationships; the possibilities are unlimited. The next chapter is a blank page, network your way into the next beautiful season of life!

QUESTIONS FOR CONSIDERATION:

What happens when life throws you curve balls? How do I react?

Am I networking without realizing it? Why do I think I am not?

Do I believe in myself?

Who is my advocate, why would that person believe in me?

Do I need a mentor or more than one?

Looking back at my life, what would I do differently? Why ?

Dr. Cherie Reynolds, (h.c.)

Don't Give Up After The First Response

How do I use the Power of the ask when I am growing my business?

Great question! Here are some key things to keep in mind when using the power of the ask:

1. Be clear about what you want: Before you ask for something, make sure you are clear about what you want. This will help you communicate your request more effectively and increase the chances of getting a positive response.

2. Be confident: Confidence is key when it comes to asking for what you want. Believe in yourself and your abilities, and don't be afraid to ask for what you deserve.

3. Be specific: When making a request, be as specific as possible. This will help the other person understand

exactly what you are asking for and increase the chances of getting a positive response.

4. Be persistent: Don't give up if you don't get the response you were hoping for. Keep asking and be persistent in your pursuit of what you want.

5. Be grateful: When someone does help you or give you what you asked for, be sure to express your gratitude. This will help build stronger relationships and increase the likelihood of future success.

Remember, the power of the ask is a valuable tool for anyone looking to improve their business. By following these key principles, you can increase your chances of success and achieve your goals.

Breaking the ice with a complete stranger can be intimidating, but there are a few things you can do to make it easier:

1. Start with a smile: A smile can go a long way in making someone feel comfortable and open to conversation. Start with a friendly smile and see how the other person responds.

2. Ask a question: Asking a question is a great way to start a conversation. It shows that you are interested in the other person and can help you find common ground. Try asking a simple question like, "How are you doing today?" or "What brings you here?"

3. Make a comment: If you notice something about the

other person or your surroundings, make a comment about it. This can be a great way to start a conversation and show that you are observant and engaged.

4. Introduce yourself: If you haven't already, introduce yourself and offer a handshake. This can help break down any barriers and make the other person feel more comfortable.

Remember, breaking the ice with a stranger can be challenging, but it's important to be confident and genuine. By showing interest in the other person and being friendly, you can create a positive first impression and start building a relationship.

When following up on a first conversation, it's important to be respectful and professional. Here are some tips for the best approach:

1. Reference the previous conversation: Start by referencing the previous conversation you had with the person. This will help jog their memory and show that you were paying attention.

2. Be specific: If you discussed any action items or next steps during your previous conversation, be sure to follow up on those specifically. This will show that you are organized and committed to following through.

3. Keep it brief: Your follow-up should be brief and to the point. Avoid going into too much detail or overwhelming the other person with information.

4. Offer value: If possible, offer something of value in your follow-up. This could be a helpful resource, a referral, or even just a kind word of encouragement.

5. End with a call to action: End your follow-up with a clear call to action. This could be a request for a follow-up meeting or a specific action item for the other person to take.

Remember, the key to a successful follow-up is to be respectful, professional, and focused on building a relationship. By following these tips, you can increase your chances of success and continue to build a strong connection with the other person.

Does the conversation end after the sale?

No, the conversation with the customer should not end after the sale. In fact, it's important to continue building a relationship with the customer even after the sale is complete. Here are some reasons why:

1. Repeat business: By continuing to engage with the customer after the sale, you increase the chances of repeat business. This can be a valuable source of revenue and help build a loyal customer base.

2. Referrals: Satisfied customers are more likely to refer others to your business. By staying in touch and building a relationship with the customer, you increase the chances of them referring others to your business.

3. Feedback: Continuing the conversation with the

customer after the sale can provide valuable feedback on your products or services. This can help you improve your offerings and better meet the needs of your customers.

4. Brand loyalty: By building a strong relationship with the customer, you can create brand loyalty. This can help differentiate your business from competitors and increase customer retention.

Remember, the conversation with the customer should be ongoing and focused on building a strong relationship. By staying in touch and providing value, you can create a loyal customer base and drive long-term success for your business.

If you're not getting a response from a client after following up, there are a few techniques you can use to try and re-engage them:

1. Change your approach: If you've been following up via email, try switching to a phone call or a different communication channel. Sometimes a different approach can help break through the noise and get a response.

2. Offer something of value: If you haven't already, try offering something of value to the client in your follow-up. This could be a helpful resource, a referral, or even just a kind word of encouragement.

3. Be persistent: Don't give up after one follow-up attempt. Be persistent and continue to follow up at regular intervals. However, be careful not to come across as pushy or aggressive.

4. Re-evaluate your message: Take a step back and re-evaluate your message. Is it clear and concise? Is it focused on the client's needs and interests? Sometimes a small tweak to your message can make a big difference in getting a response.

5. Move on: If you've tried all of the above and still haven't received a response, it may be time to move on. Don't waste too much time and energy on a client who isn't responding. Instead, focus on building relationships with other potential clients who may be more responsive.

Remember, the key to a successful follow-up is to be respectful, professional, and focused on building a relationship. By using these techniques, you can increase your chances of success and continue to build strong connections with your clients.

How to use social media in business...an example using my business

1. Social Media Marketing: Use social media platforms like Facebook, Instagram, and LinkedIn to promote your solar business to realtors. Create engaging content that highlights the benefits of solar energy and how it can help realtors save money on their energy bills.

2. Referral Program: Offer a referral program to realtors who refer their clients to your solar business. This can be a win-win situation for both parties, as the realtor can earn a commission for each referral, while you get new customers without any investment.

3. Networking: Attend local real estate events and conferences to network with realtors and build relationships. Offer to speak at these events and share your knowledge about solar energy and its benefits.

4. Online Advertising: Use online advertising platforms like Google AdWords and Facebook Ads to target realtors in your area. Create ads that highlight the benefits of solar energy and how it can help realtors save money on their energy bills.

5. Content Marketing: Create blog posts, videos, and other content that educates realtors about solar energy and its benefits. Share this content on social media and other online platforms to attract realtors to your business.

6. Partnership with Solar Installers: Partner with solar installers in your area to offer realtors a complete solar energy solution. This can help you attract more realtors to your business without any investment.

7. Free Consultation: Offer a free consultation to realtors to help them understand how solar energy can benefit their business. This can be a great way 9to build relationships and attract new customers without any investment.

I have been in the business building Space for 25 years after I left my Corporate Job at Hobart Corporation! I love introducing a new product after research and due diligence to my warm market as well as new markets! I prefer in person connections versus online but due to the current standards I know we can get results as long as we are persistent and consistent! Videos and showing your Smiling face is known to be the most effective! Happy Selling and be Confident, you have to use "The Power of the Ask!"

QUESTIONS FOR CONSIDERATION:

Am I clear and specific about "my ask" ?

Do I show / express gratitude when someone helps me?

How can I start building a relationship with someone I met for the first time at a networking event?

When I first meet someone do I express interest in their business? How can I benefit if I just give them an appetizer to my business versus the entree!

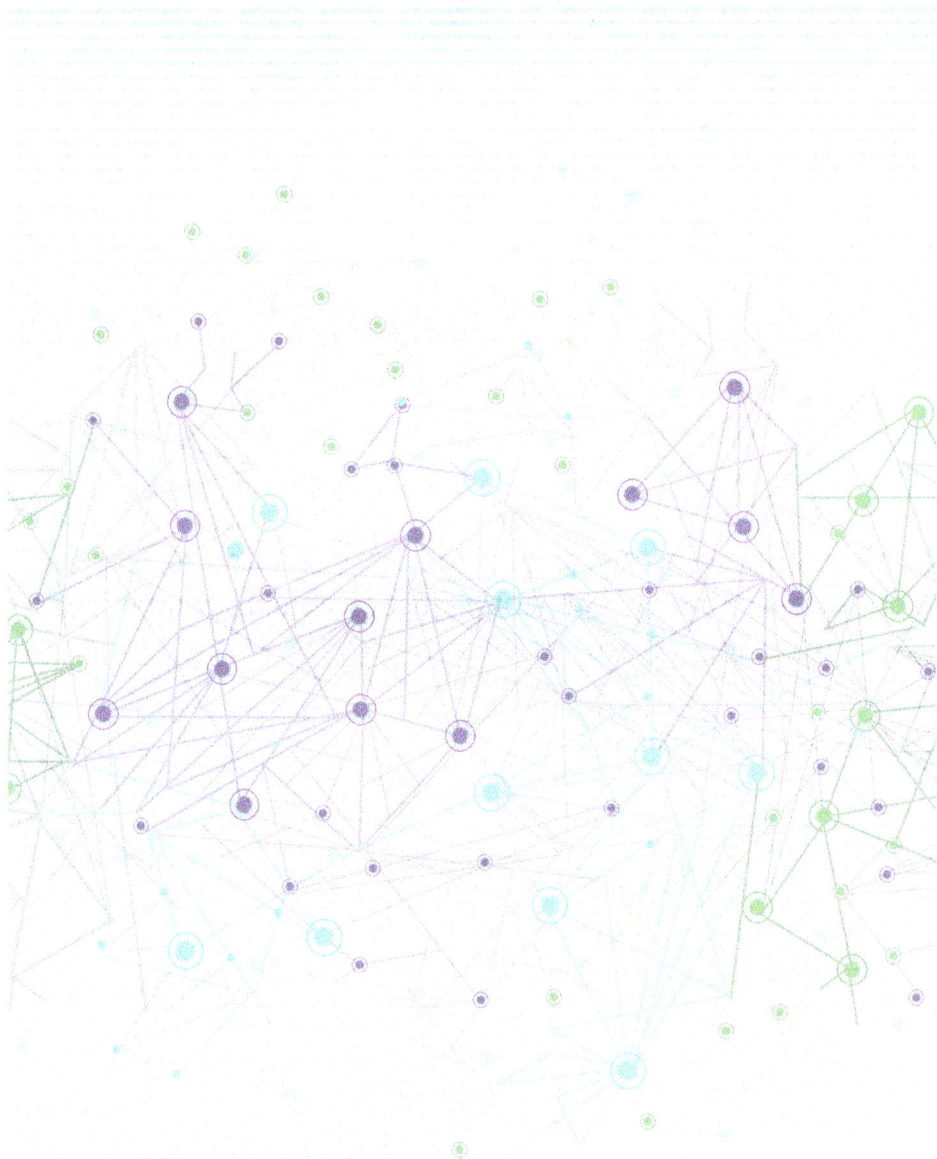

Arvee Robinson

Make An Impact With Networking

"What do you do?" I asked a young lady. "Blah, blah, blah," she rambled on endlessly. Somebody come and save me! I thought to myself. By the time she finished, I didn't have a clue as to what she did. That's a real problem when attending networking meetings. Many savvy business owners don't know how to say what they do in a way that is beneficial to the listener. Nor are they clear as to the services they provide to their customers. Consequently, they don't attract any new business and their networking efforts are wasted.

It doesn't have to be that way. With a little training and practice, you can make a positive impact and attract a steady stream of clients every time you walk into a networking event.

Networking with strangers is not an easy task. We were not born with the knowledge of how to approach people we don't know. As a matter of fact, your parents probably told you repeatedly, *"Don't talk to strangers!"* Now, as adults you are expected to go against your inner core teachings. There is hope, however.

I have led networking meetings for over two decades. I have served as the leader of professional networking groups consisting of corporate executives, entrepreneurs, and service providers. As well as smaller private women's organizations and Christian networking groups. Even though they are all different, they all have one common theme. People attend because they want to give and get business. Period. They leave when they don't receive referrals, prospects, or leads. Thinking that it is the organizations' fault or its members. In reality, it is solely their responsibility. They just don't know how to make a lasting impression, much less create impact.

I'm going to teach you six ways that you can make a huge impact every time you attend a networking function. This will expand into more business, connections, and opportunities.

We are going to use the acronym **IMPACT.**

I stands for **Interested.** When you meet new people whether at a networking meeting or any other event, be interested instead of interesting. Show your interest by being curious and asking them questions about their business. Act as though you can't learn enough about them in the short time you have together. By embracing this approach, you can also learn whether or not they are a good candidate for your services. Remember, not everyone is your ideal client. This can be a fast and polite way to eliminate those who aren't.

M stands for **Message**. What are you saying when someone asks you, "What do you do?" This is the million-dollar question, and it is asked at everyone networking function. Yet, many business owners do not have the right answer. When asked, they often answer with great difficultly or they open the flood gates and begin to slime the very people they are trying to impress. Instead, take your answer seriously by preparing it ahead of time. Know what you are going to say, make it benefit driven, and practice it so it rows off your tongue quickly and easily.

P stands for **Plan**. Before you attend a networking event, do your research, and find out who is going to attend. Decide ahead of time who you want to connect with and look for them at the event. If you want to make certain they are going to be there, contact them ahead of time by phone, text, or email and simply ask them. Another powerful technique is to call and invite them to ride with you to the event. This way you will have personal time with them to build trust and rapport and even create a new friendship.

A stands for **Action**. Take massive action at every networking opportunity. Get there early and leave late. Make a commitment to participate in whatever activities are happening during that time. Be fully prepared and present. During my many years of networking, I've seen people run into an event at the last minute, talk to a few of their friends and leave. Later, they wonder why they didn't get any new business. If you are going to take the time, spend the money, and eat the rubber chicken, you might as well make every minute count. Also, don't hang out with your friends. Greet them and move on and meet people you don't already know. Create a game for yourself and try to meet ten or twenty new people at every networking event. Once you meet someone new, don't stay too long. Make the connection and move on. You can politely excuse yourself by using this script, "I know there are people you want to meet and so do I, it was great meeting you, I will contact you tomorrow to set up a meeting." Confidently shake their hand and go and find another person you don't know.

C stands for **Calendar**. When you meet someone that you are interested in doing business with, don't just get their business card and contact them later. This may have worked in the past, however, today it is no longer effective, and you will spend hours spinning your wheels trying to get hold of them. Instead, schedule them on your calendar while they are present in front of you. Most business owners have a calendar app on their phone and can access it quickly. Have them commit to a meeting while they are excited about meeting you. Or you can always schedule yourself on their calendar. Either way, it is a firm commitment to a future meeting.

T stands for **Touch**. Now it is time to follow up to get the business. Nowadays people are extremely busy, and life is full of distractions. To make an impression it is important to follow up immediately after contacting your prospective client and to do so at least seven times. That's what it takes, seven touches. The old saying, '*The fortune is in the follow-up,*" holds true here so keep following up until they either buy or die. Most business owners give up after only one or two touches. Consequently, they don't get the business because the warm lead quickly turned cold.

There are many ways today that you can connect to a prospect after a networking event. The first one and the most ideal is to schedule a meeting on each other's calendar during the event. If not, send them a quick video sharing how much you enjoyed meeting them and that you look forward to scheduling time with them in the future. Other techniques include a quick, text, email, or phone message. If you have their address, send a handwritten card written in blue ink. This is a great way to get someone's attention. If you have difficulty contacting someone, try reaching out using social media. Many business owners are on LinkedIn and other popular sites. Multiple touches work best so keep connecting. Think of creative ways to reach out that will make someone smile and remember you.

Use these six simple techniques to make a positive impact on potential clients, business connections, and power partners and they will last a lifetime. Networking is an art. It takes skill, persistence, and practice. Once you learn what works best you will make a lasting impact.

QUESTIONS FOR CONSIDERATION:

What is the impact when I meet a new person? Do I find them to be interesting or in leave them interested in knowing more about my services/ products?

When asked what do I do for business, can I be clear, concise, and specific?

Do I prepare myself before going into a meeting by practicing my introduction?

How many times do I make a connection with a new prospect?

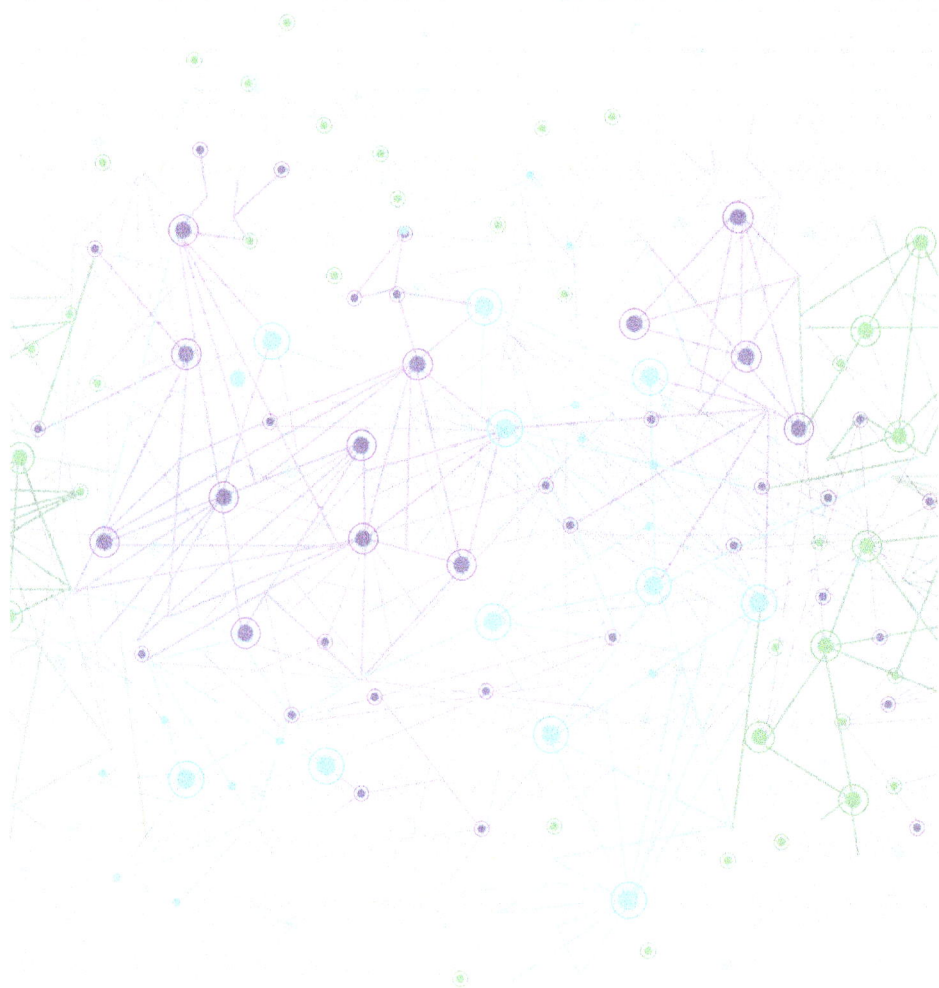

Dr. Avic Ronquillo De Castro (h.c.)

The Essentials of Bookkeeping In Business

I've been doing bookkeeping for years and connecting with people (personal & businesses). My ask is for you is to refer me businesses or professionals who may need my services. I wrote this article as my way of giving back to the community, the world & my friends & family to share my knowledge.

Bookkeeping is the process of recording and organizing financial transactions of a business. Proper bookkeeping is essential for maintaining accurate financial records and making informed business decisions. Here are some key essentials in bookkeeping:

Record Transactions: All financial transactions, including sales, purchases, expenses, and payments, must be accurately recorded. This can be done manually or using accounting software.

Chart of Accounts: Create a structured list of accounts that categorize transactions. This helps organize and track various types of income, expenses, assets, liabilities, and equity.

Double-Entry System: Use the double-entry accounting system, where each transaction affects at least two accounts with equal and opposite entries. This system helps maintain the accounting equation (Assets = Liabilities + Equity).

Invoicing and Receipts: Issue invoices to customers for products or services provided and keep records of sales receipts. This is crucial for tracking revenue and accounts receivable.

Expense Tracking: Keep track of all business expenses, including receipts for purchases, bills, and payments. This ensures accurate expense reporting and helps with tax deductions.

Bank Reconciliation: Regularly reconcile bank statements with your accounting records to identify any discrepancies or errors. This helps ensure that all transactions are accurately recorded.

Petty Cash Management: If your business uses petty cash for small expenses, maintain a separate record for these transactions and ensure proper documentation. Separate your personal transactions from your business transactions. Always use your business bank account for all your business transactions.

Financial Statements: Generate regular financial statements, including the income statement, balance sheet, and cash flow statement. These statements provide a clear overview of your business's financial health.

Accrual vs. Cash Basis: Decide whether to use the accrual basis of accounting (recording transactions when they occur, regardless of cash flow) or the cash basis (recording transactions when cash changes hands). The choice impacts when revenue and expenses are recognized.

Backup and Security: Keep backups of your financial records to prevent data loss. If using accounting software, implement security measures to protect sensitive financial information. Keep all expenses receipts as backups.

Consistency: Maintain consistency in your bookkeeping practices. Use standardized naming conventions, account codes, and recording methods to ensure clarity and accuracy.

Documentation: Maintain proper documentation for all transactions. This includes invoices, receipts, contracts, and any other supporting documents.

Tax Compliance: Ensure your bookkeeping practices align with tax regulations in your jurisdiction. Keep records needed for tax reporting and filings.

Periodic Reviews: Regularly review your financial records to catch errors, identify trends, and make informed decisions for your business.

If you are a hands-on self-employed worker, you can buy a software that suits your needs like QuickBooks PRO desktop or online.

Professional Help: If needed, consider consulting with a certified accountant or bookkeeper who are knowledgeable to ensure accuracy and compliance with financial regulations.

Proper bookkeeping provides the foundation for financial reporting, analysis, and decision-making. It's crucial for both small and large businesses to maintain accurate and organized financial records.

QUESTIONS FOR CONSIDERATION:

Why is bookkeeping important to my business?

Do I need to hire a bookkeeper?

Will knowing my financial status help me make better business decisions?

Dr. Kaye Sheffield (h.c), M.S., CCC-SLP

The Value of Networking – To Know Yourself

I am sitting in my beautiful, giving backyard, so thankful for the provisions of peaches, nectarines, lettuce, herbs, squash, and so many more. Some are ready to give of their fruit and share. And some are not so ready! I am so thankful for the friends that I have and remembering how important and giving relationships are for each of us. Some are willing to give of their fruit and share, and some are not so ready.

Since agreeing to write about Networking, I have wondered, what is networking in the true sense of the word and how does it impact each of our lives.

Networking?? Networking is us! It is Life, how we operate, move, socialize, and give. "The happiest people in the world are the givers, the generous people." As John Maxwell says, …"we are created to be generous, to share and to help one another." That is networking!

Networking is making connections and building relationships. It allows you to learn what worked for them/others and what didn't work, to gain advice and recommendations, and to receive feedback. In the best networking situations, it is beneficial to both parties.

In reading about networking, I have learned that there is true value in networking, no matter what Area of Networking you are doing it in, whether you are doing it Personally (Personal Area of Networking), Locally (Local Area Networking), in your community/city/Metropolitan area (MAN), or in a Wide area (WAN). It increases your visibility, your reputation, your trust from others, and it can increase your business growth and build more impactful connections.

Personally, I find that we network everyday with friends, neighbors, family, at the gym, library, taking classes, working, eating out, traveling, and at the places that we frequent. And it is really difficult when we are unable to network due to an illness, medical concern, pandemic, or have a lack of provisions such as, a phone, computer, or car.

I have found that you really learn and know more about yourself when you network with others. The more giving that you are, the more generous that you become. What a beautiful way to live, by showing up at events, reaching out to others, and being willing to share. I have found that there are Five "C"s to networking, whether it is personal or business:

1. **Concern:** If you have an interest or concern for another person, or for people in general, you are able to relate to them. Sometimes it is a helpful attitude that you have to pick up on something that you see or hear. We ask questions to understand their concern(s) more fully.

2. **Communicate:** As you hear what the other person is saying, with concern in your heart, you begin to communicate and share with them. Many people share with a helpful and caring heart the things that they have found helpful and safe for them.

3. **Confide:** Many times, in talking with others and networking, people will confide and share what they know. It may be the things that are deep in their heart, or those things that aren't shared with others except on rare occasions. It may be things that they are embarrassed to share.

4. **Capsule:** of information that you have heard them say, and sharing what you know about their concerns. You can say, "I understood you to say___" as you capsule the concerns, they shared with you. You are communicating and confiding in each other. It is a special time, and you are learning more about yourself in the sharing.

5. **Connected:** You are connected in your networking with that person, and you want to stay connected in the future. The networking that you did in person, a phone conversation, or on a zoom call, is special and you will want to stay connected and share how you are doing and how the network time helped you.

In our day to day sharing times (networking) with others we: 1. **Listen** and understand. 2. **Learn** from each other. 3. **Love** is shared. 4. **Laugh** with them. 5. **Leave** with the connection that we just established together and carry forward this connection until another day.

This seems so easy to do and yet it can be so complicated for someone for whom the idea of networking does not come to easily. There are people who are difficult to converse/network with. Those that want to only talk about themselves, and those who don't want to share thoughts and ideas, or to learn from each other. These times are really difficult, and we can only give an idea, or plant a seed, that the other person may think about later. That is one reason why it is so important to stay connected and talk with that person again.

Networking is for everyone, and on a daily basis.

If we are interested in being entrepreneurs and organizing a business, then Networking is even more important for us to do and to do well. We need to work with others and operate in an organized and caring manner and be willing to risk loss in order to make money. Networking and being an entrepreneur go hand in hand. It is an adventure.

In order to become stronger in networking and to increase your/our entrepreneurship, you/we need to do several things:

1. Build relationships with people.

2. Keep in contact with the people that we have built

relationships with.

3. Make an influential connection by building trust with that contact.

4. Stay positive. Try to find the positive in most things.

5. Improve your communication skills through zoom, 3-way calls, emailing, and social media.

6. Have no expectations for outcomes.

7. Focus on your efforts to Listen, Learn, Laugh, and Love.

8. Make your communication skills flexible and keep learning.

So how do you get started? 1. Start with who you know, family and friends, or groups that you are a part of. 2. Seek out new opportunities to network and share. 3. Talk to people wherever you are, standing in line, going through TSA for a flight, at a restaurant, and so many more places. 4. Be open to meeting new people. 5. Be curious and ask questions. 6. Have a sense of humor and talk about what is happening around you. 7. Follow up, exchange email or cell phone information, and stay in contact. 8. Offer to send them something or give them information, a video, a talk that is pertinent. 9. Prepare and have a plan for Follow-up, and what you want to achieve. 10. Think about your network beyond an event, and always Follow-up. 11. Ask if they know someone who would like the information that you are sharing. 12. Build up the trust between the two parties. If you say that you are going to do something or send them something, do it as quickly as possible—this builds trust.

The most important thing to know about networking is to put a SMILE on your face and to be POSITIVE. Remember to be a GIVER---They are the Happiest people in the world.

QUESTIONS FOR CONSIDERATION:

When networking am I a good listener or a good talker?

How is networking valuable to you?

What could you share with others that you feel good about because you benefited from that experience?

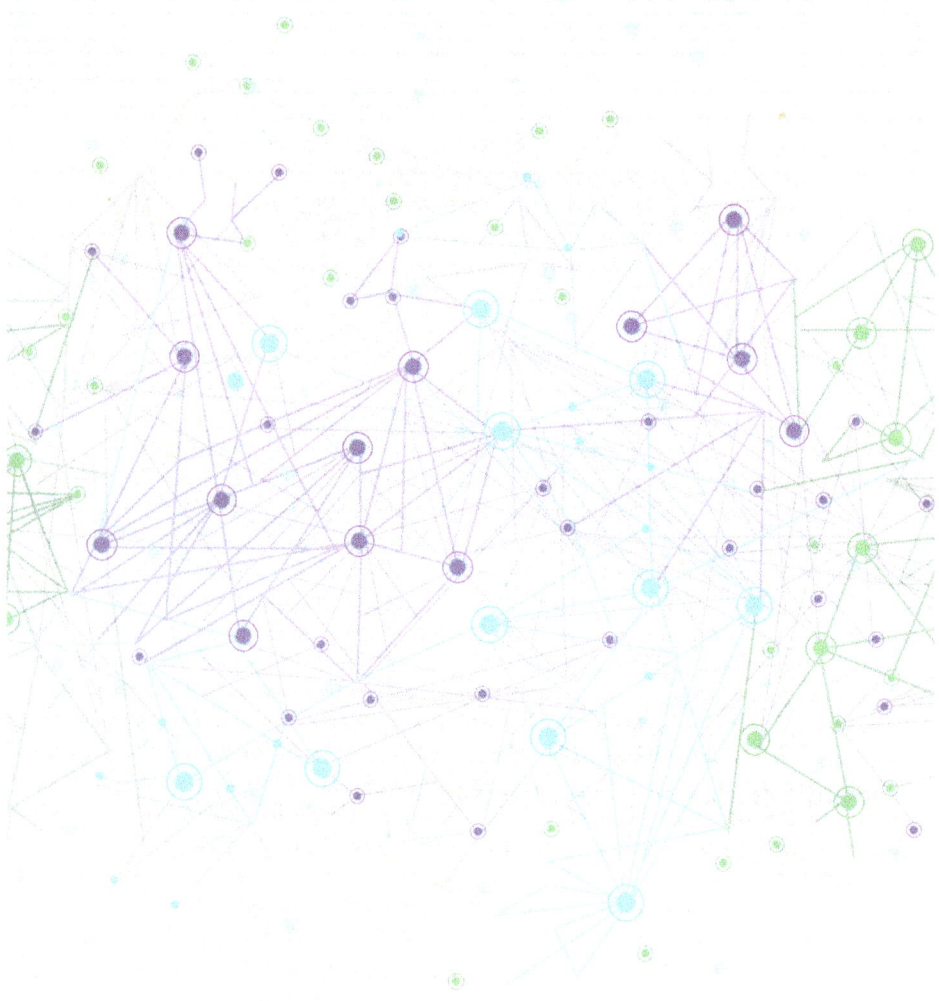

† Dr. Deborah Thorne (h.c.)

Mastering Follow Up

Constantly seeking avenues to enhance my skills and abilities is non-negotiable. Whether it involves soliciting feedback from others, self-reflection, or acquiring new knowledge, I am always committed to growth and development. This approach enables me to deliver top-notch assistance and service.

I am sharing this information to emphasize the importance of follow-up and how to execute it effectively. First, mastering the process means having a thorough understanding and control over it. Follow-ups refer to keeping in touch with customers, leads, and prospects. Customers have already purchased our products or services, leads are potential customers we interact with, and prospects are individuals who are most likely to buy from us, including our ideal clients.

My goal for this chapter is that you will have a more transparent comprehension of follow-up and some practical tactics that you can implement right away.

As the famous motivational speaker Jim Rohn said, "The fortune is in the follow-up." That's why it's crucial to follow up on things. I have a few questions: How many follow-ups do you usually do? Who do you follow up with? And how often do you follow up? Here are some statistics from the National Sales Executive Association

Can you believe it, 48% of salespeople never follow up with a lead? You know that stack of business cards you collected at different events and promised to get in touch with those people, that's part of that 48%. How many potential customers are in that stack of business cards?

Did you know establishing a solid relationship with potential customers is essential for successful sales? Surprisingly, only 10% of salespeople make more than three contacts, but between the fifth and twelfth contact is when 80% of people make their purchase.

It's also important to note that if you or your business is not in contact with someone for 30 days, you lose 10% of your recognizability. This means they might forget about you and your business in less than a year. Remember, people prefer doing business with people they know, like, trust, and remember!

Do you spend most of your time searching for new people to network with or following up with previous clients? While networking events can be great for meeting new people, building rapport and relationships with them takes time.

On the other hand, your previous clients already know, like, and trust you, but have you helped them remember you? Did they hear from you after you made that sale, or is the only communication they get from you is more offers to buy? What is your customer's sales journey?

Often, people make the mistake of jumping straight into sales talk when meeting a potential business contact. For example, after scheduling a one-on-one conversation, they may bombard the other person with information about their products and services, expecting an immediate sale. However, this approach rarely works and often leads to disappointment.

Instead, follow-up should focus on building a relationship with the other person. Just like in dating, asking someone to marry you on the first date is not advisable. It's better to take the time to get to know them and allow them to get to know you so you can determine if there is a potential for a future business partnership.

In my chapter, I aim to share the skills and tactics to help you become a Master of Follow-up and incorporate these strategies into your business acumen.

We have discussed the reasons for follow-up, and now, let's explore the forms that follow-up can take. Follow-up encompasses any activity that puts you and your business before past and potential customers. It is important to remember that your current customers are better buyers because they already know, like, and trust you. Therefore, it is your responsibility to help them remember you.

The first step is to ensure that your product or service is of optimal quality. Take an honest look at what you provide and how you provide it. Then, write down what makes your product or service the best available.

If you are unsure about the quality of your product or service, ask your customers for feedback. A helpful evaluation question is: "On a scale of 1 to 10, 10 being the best, how would you rate our product or service?" If they do not give you a 10, ask them what you can do to improve and get a ten from them. This way, your customers will tell you what they expect, and you can also identify other product or service needs they may have.

An evaluation is a form of follow-up, and you can include a note thanking your customers for their purchase.

Follow-ups help to keep your name and business in front of your customers, which improves their customer journey and keeps you top of mind when they need the product or service you provide. It is important to note that not every follow-up is a request to buy. Instead, focus on nurturing the relationship by using follow-ups to stay connected with your customers. People buy from those they know, like, trust, and remember. Here are some examples of follow-ups that can help nurture relationships:

- Acknowledging birthdays
- Acknowledging anniversaries
- Announcing new products

- Announcing new services
- Company newsletter
- Company podcast
- Company blog
- Relevant articles
- Media information
- Social media
- Groups
- Events
- Virtual events
- Collaborations
- Books
- eBooks
- Staying quiet in networking groups, not providing service, or letting people know who you are

Businesses of all sizes can benefit from using modern technology to implement effective tactics. For instance, you can join my birthday circle and receive a Happy Birthday by visiting TheDivasBirthdayCircle.com, and I'll be able to celebrate your special day. It's an example of nurturing contact.

Most businesses, regardless of size, can use these tactics with the assistance of modern technology.

Although, as previously stated, following up with current customers is the most effective, many of us continue to reach out to new prospects instead. This can be valuable when done the right way. There are many in-person and virtual networking events held weekly. Let's discuss seven mistakes that keep us from making the most of these events.

We attend our regular events, made up of people we know already. Although this may feel more comfortable, it doesn't allow us to make new contacts. People who may use our products or services or people who may know people who may use our products or services.

- We attend meetings involving people in the same business rather than the meetings that our ideal customers would attend.

- We provide the same "30-second introduction" week after week, never addressing the needs and concerns of the audience.

- We tend to sit back and socialize rather than actively network.

- We repeat the same information in the "chat, " failing to address the audience in attendance and how we might support them.

- We fail to follow up with new attendees.

- We fail to have written intentions or goals for our meetings.

There are various ways technology and virtual assistants can assist you in completing tasks. By focusing on the right things, you can increase your productivity. As for me, here are some tools I rely on to enhance my networking skills:

- Virtual assistant: I engage a service provider from outside the US. It is noteworthy that I only assign them simple, routine tasks.

- CRM Contact Relationship Manager: My preferred CRM tool enables me to send emails, flyers, text messages, and more.

- Zoom engagement tool: This tool is useful in monitoring the Zoom meetings I attend, keeping track of the chats, and reminding me to follow up.

- I also use greeting cards and gifts to follow up with my clients and prospects automatically.

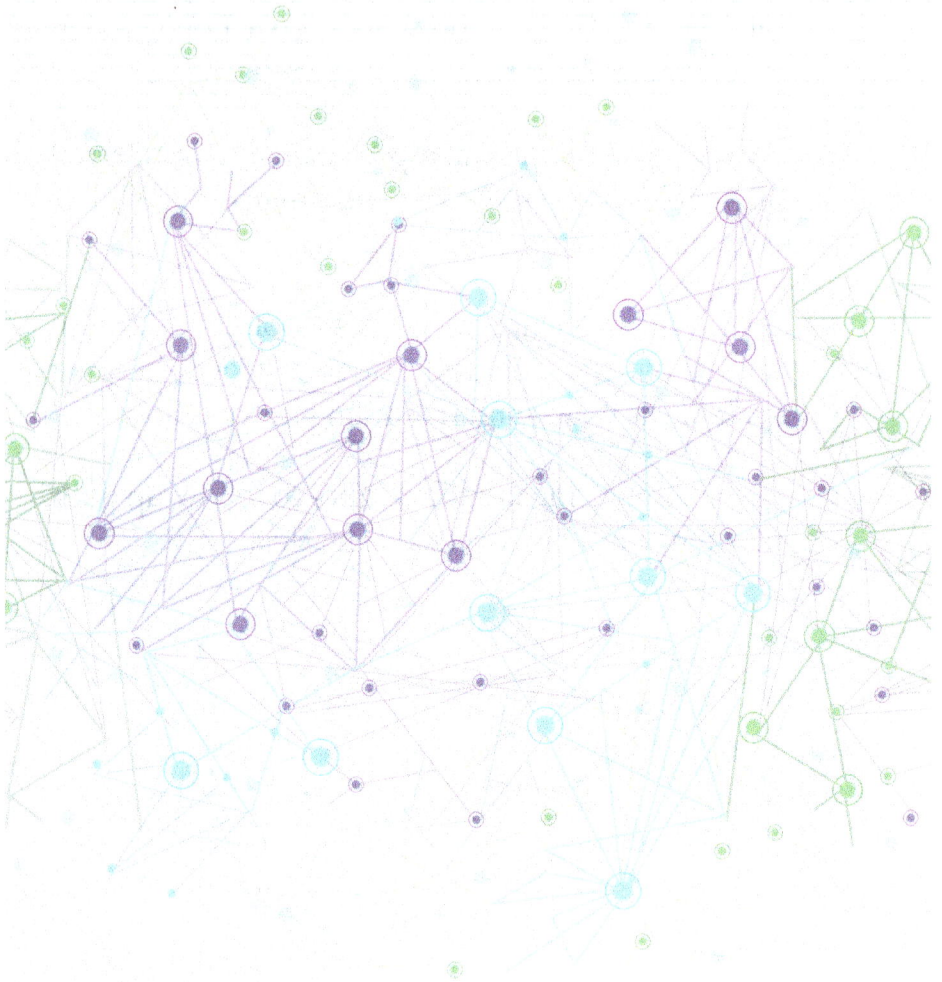

Angel Toussaint

The Right Business & Networking For The Recipient

I am a natural personal networker because I love meeting and talking with people. I am an extrovert personality that knows no strangers. Many years ago, I had a very close friend say every time I meet someone new after a few minutes it seems like we have known each other for years. I enjoy getting to know people, learning about their backgrounds, ambitions, and goals.

However, when I decided to become an entrepreneur networking was not so easy. I found it difficult to covert my network of people into customers or even potential customers. I learned after several entrepreneurial ventures my network was not the issue and I needed to change my mode of networking.

When I am networking on a personal level it is easy to connect. In conversation I always seem to find things we have in common and phone numbers are exchanged, lunches and get togethers are planned and fun just flows.

When networking for business I just did not have the same enthusiasm. I found it difficult to have a "sales pitch." I found it difficult to speak with enthusiasm about my product or service. I have close connections in my personal network that would buy my product or service simply to support me, but that network is not large enough to sustain a business or to help promote business growth. I was plagued with the negative association of being a sales person. I always thought of the sales people as the pushy sales person you practically have to beat off with a baseball bat before they will accept the word "no" or "not interested" and I did not want to be that person. Then one day I was at a workshop and one of the speakers said what I needed to hear.

We are all sales people; we are sales people every day we just do not recognize it. When you watch a good movie, you tell your friends to watch it. You give them just enough information so they want to watch it, but you don't give them too much information or it will ruin the movie for them. Why do you want them to see the movie? It is because you thought they would enjoy it and you look forward to hearing what they thought of it, and if they enjoyed it as much as you thought they would. You want to discuss the results and feelings about the movie with them. The same principle applies to good books, services, and products. Social media platforms like Nextdoor are loaded with neighborhood referrals. People who have enjoyed the benefits of a product or service and they want to share it with all their neighbors including neighbors they have never met.

For me, building a professional network to grow a business which is full of satisfied customers and new customers was quite different from building a personal network. I discovered, in order for me to grow a professional network I needed to know if my product or service was truly beneficial to the recipient. I have always been a product of my product or service and if I didn't see or feel a benefit myself it was impossible for me to be enthusiastic when presenting my product or service to others.

I have had many people try to help me grow a business. I knew success was possible because I saw the success of those around me. As I attempted to apply the tactics and strategies people were sharing with me I would get frustrated when I saw no growth. I was convinced I did not have what it took to succeed in direct sales of any product or service. However, I didn't want to keep working for someone else for the rest of my days on planet earth, so I continued my quest to become a successful entrepreneur.

The quest has been long and exhausting, but the following words and mindsets always helped me keep going:

- If at first you don't succeed, try again, and again,
- Never give up
- If they can do it you can do it
- Where there is a will there is a way
- Failure is just a stepping stone to success

So, I kept attending webinars, seminars, workshops, public speaking events, etc. and each time I would pick up a little something to hold on to that kept my entrepreneurial dream alive. Attending these functions always offset the words I would hear from people telling me it is never going to happen just give up.

I tried many different types of businesses, and as I failed I would always remind myself of what I learned. I focused on the belief that each failure was preparing me for my future success, and it was.

In one workshop I attended, a speaker shared these words, you will know your business is right for you when you don't want to do anything else. Those words rang absolutely true when I found the business I am in now.

In all my past endeavors, if a new business opportunity were presented to me I would easily give up on what I was doing and move forward to see what the new business opportunity would bring my way. New opportunities are like raindrops and if your current business is an umbrella full of holes then the raindrops will dampen you. If a business is right for you, it is like a solid waterproof umbrella protecting you from the hundreds and hundreds of falling raindrops.

I knew I found the right business for me, and it is confirmed every time a new business opportunity or new idea is presented to me. I am not distracted from my current path, and I have no desire to look in any other direction.

The joy I feel when a customer shares their positive alarming results from using my products has completely patched every hole in my business umbrella and new business opportunities are no longer a distraction. Now I am networking for the recipients' benefits from my product, not for the fastest deposit to my wallet. It is amazing how much easier it is for me to network for business. It is no longer the strenuous task it was in the past. Networking for the recipient has made business networking as easy and enjoyable as personal networking.

Building a network is work, you should be willing to do the work. You should also be excited about the work you are doing. If you find you cannot be excited about any aspect of your work you either need to hire out the portion or portions you dread or you may need to examine whether or not the business is right for you.

I believe in the EFW (exposure, follow up, willingness) method for business networking.

- Exposure is everything – if your business is not being exposed to massive amounts of people then you will not grow. This requires marketing usually in more than one form. Do as much marketing as your budget will allow.

- Fortune is in the Follow up – when you get feedback from your exposure you have to be in a position to properly follow up. Follow up does not always mean talking about closing a sale. Follow up means keeping that connection alive. Call and just check in see how the person is doing ask about their life, show an interest in them as a person not just as your potential customer.

- Work with the willing – when a person says no or they are not interested thank them for their time, thank them for listening and wish them a pleasant day. If a person responses in a foul manner apologize for upsetting them and move on. Remember the world can be harsh for people so calendar them for a possible follow up in a year. No or not interested can mean no not interested now, that doesn't mean forever. People's circumstances change as much as the weather does. What was ugly today may not be there tomorrow. Be kink in the face of unkindness. Be calm in a storm. Don't take it personally, remember it is never personal when dealing with a stranger, why, because strangers don't know you.

Networking can be fun when you have the right attitude and right tools to make it a successful part of your business. You should never stop networking in your business or personal life. Networking means adding new people and new information to your life. Networking is connecting and connection is the foundation of relationships and relationships are the foundation of human life. As I was writing this chapter there were two people who I wanted to acknowledge with a special thanks:

Coralean Chavis for sticking with me through venture after venture looking for the product or service that would capture my heart and propel me forward in my quest to be a happy successful entrepreneur. She saw my drive and determination and she didn't allow me to give up or to live with the negative attitude that sometimes surfaces when people discourage you.

Joan Wakeland for her continued support and encouragement no matter what direction I was going. She shared words of wisdom and helped me learn patience and better listening skills.

My deepest gratitude to these two women.

QUESTIONS FOR CONSIDERATION:

Building a network is work! How will that work benefit you in your pursuit of achieving your goals?

How receptive are you to new opportunities?

Why do individuals tend to jump from one business to another?

When will you know the business you are building is right for you?

Are you avoiding being a sales person?

Dr. Dorothy Wolons (h.c.)

Networking With Charisma

Networking rooms can be intimidating, especially if you're trying to make a good impression on the people you meet. However, with a few tips and tricks, you can command attention and exude charisma in any networking environment. Here are some strategies to help you confidently engage with others and make meaningful connections.

Have a positive attitude

One of the most important things you can do to command attention and charisma in a networking room is to have a positive attitude. People are drawn to those who are happy, friendly, and approachable. So, when you walk into the room, make a conscious effort to smile, be upbeat, and exude confidence. Remember that everyone in the room is there for the same reason you are - to meet new people and make connections - so approach them with a positive mindset and a can-do attitude.

Dress appropriately

The way you present yourself is also important when it comes to commanding charisma in a networking room. Dress appropriately for the occasion, and make sure your attire is both professional and comfortable. You want to feel confident and at ease in your clothing, so choose something that makes you look and feel your best.

Start with a strong opening line

When you approach someone new in a networking room, start with a strong opening line. This could be a compliment, a question about their work, or a shared interest. The key is to be confident and engaging from the start. For example, you might say, "I really enjoyed your presentation earlier. I was wondering if you might have a few minutes to chat about your work in more detail?"

Listen actively

When you're having a conversation with someone, be sure to listen actively. This means giving your full attention to the person you're speaking with, and showing genuine interest in what they have to say. Ask questions, offer insights, and engage in a back-and-forth dialogue that shows you value their input. People are more likely to remember those who show an interest in them and their work, so make sure you're giving the person you're speaking with your undivided attention.

Be genuine and authentic

Charisma is often associated with confidence and charm, but it's important to remember that authenticity is key. Be true to yourself and don't try to be someone you're not in order to impress others. People can sense when you're being fake, so focus on being genuine and authentic in your interactions. This will help you build trust and credibility with those you meet and make it more likely that they'll want to work with you in the future.

Follow up

After you've made a connection with someone in a networking room, be sure to follow up with them. This could mean sending an email, connecting on LinkedIn, or scheduling a coffee meeting to discuss potential collaborations. By taking the initiative to follow up, you show that you're serious about building a relationship with the person, and that you value their time and expertise.

Practice, practice, practice

Finally, the more you practice networking, the more confident and charismatic you'll become. Attend networking events regularly and try to meet new people and build relationships. Over time, you'll become more comfortable in these situations, and your charisma and networking skills will improve.

Commanding charisma in a networking room is all about projecting confidence, positivity, and authenticity. By dressing appropriately, starting with a strong opening line, listening actively, and following up with those you meet, you can build strong connections and make a lasting impression on the people you encounter. So, go forth and network with confidence - you've got this!

Best ways to be remembered after a networking event or social event

Networking events and social events can be great opportunities to meet new people, make connections, and build relationships. However, it's not always easy to stand out in a crowded room, and it can be hard to make a lasting impression on the people you meet. Here are some tips on how to be remembered after a networking or social event:

Follow up promptly

One of the best ways to be remembered after a networking or social event is to follow up with the people you met. Send a personalized email or message within 24-48 hours of the event, thanking them for their time and expressing your interest in staying in touch. This shows that you're serious about building a relationship, and it keeps you top of mind.

Add value

Another way to be remembered is to add value to the people you meet. This could mean sending them an article or resource that relates to their work, introducing them to someone in your network who might be able to help them, or offering to collaborate on a project together.

When you add value to someone's life, they're more likely to remember you and want to work with you in the future.

Be authentic

People are more likely to remember those who are authentic and genuine. Be true to yourself, and don't try to be someone you're not in order to impress others. Share your passions, interests, and experiences in a way that is honest and authentic and listen actively to what others have to say. When you're genuine, people are more likely to remember you and want to work with you.

Have a unique story

Having a unique story or perspective can also help you stand out and be remembered. Share your personal or professional journey, and what led you to attend the event. Talk about your passions, interests, or experiences that set you apart from others. When you have a compelling story, people are more likely to remember you and want to learn more.

Be present and engaged

Finally, be present and engaged during the event. Put your phone away, make eye contact, and actively listen to what others have to say. Show a genuine interest in the people you meet and make an effort to connect with them on a personal level. When you're fully present and engaged, people are more likely to remember you and want to work with you.

Being remembered after a networking or social event is all about following up promptly, adding value, being authentic, having a unique story, and being present and engaged. By implementing these tips, you can make a lasting impression on the people you meet and build strong relationships that will benefit you in the future.

How to attract the right customers at a networking event

Attracting the right customers at a networking event can be challenging, but there are several strategies you can use to increase your chances of success. Here are some tips on how to attract the right customers at a networking event:

Define your target audience

Before attending a networking event, it's essential to define your target audience. Who are the customers you want to attract? What are their interests, needs, and pain points? Knowing your target audience will help you tailor your messaging and approach to attract the right customers.

Prepare a clear and compelling elevator pitch

Your elevator pitch should be concise, memorable, and focused on the benefits you offer to your target customers. Be clear about what you do, who you serve, and how you can help solve their problems. Use language that resonates with your target audience and highlights your unique value proposition.

Set goals and objectives

Before attending a networking event, set specific goals and objectives for what you want to achieve. Do you want to meet a certain number of potential customers, generate leads, or make sales? Having a clear focus will help you stay motivated and focused throughout the event.

Be visible and approachable

Make yourself visible and approachable at the networking event. Wear a name tag, stand in a visible location, and make eye contact with people. Be friendly, smile, and make small talk. Ask questions and show a genuine interest in others. This will help you make connections with potential customers and build rapport.

Offer value

One of the best ways to attract the right customers is to offer value. Share your knowledge, expertise, or resources with others. Offer free samples, demos, or consultations. Provide tips and insights that can help potential customers solve their problems. When you offer value, you'll build trust and credibility with your target audience, which can lead to long-term relationships and referrals.

Follow up promptly

Finally, follow up promptly with the potential customers you meet at the networking event. Send a personalized email or message within 24-48 hours of the event, thanking them for their time and expressing your interest in working with them. Be specific about how you can help them solve their problems and add value to their lives. This will show that you're serious about building a relationship and help you stand out from the crowd.

Attracting the right customers at a networking event requires preparation, focus, and a customer-centric approach. Define your target audience, prepare a clear and compelling elevator pitch, set goals and objectives, be visible and approachable, offer value, and follow up promptly. By implementing these tips, you'll increase your chances of attracting the right customers and building strong relationships that will benefit your business in the long run.

Best way to write an elevator speech and its purpose for a networking event

An elevator speech, also known as an elevator pitch, is a brief, persuasive speech that's designed to spark interest in what you do, who you serve, and how you can help solve a problem. It's called an elevator speech because it's meant to be short enough to deliver during the time it takes to ride an elevator, usually 30 seconds to 2 minutes.

The purpose of an elevator speech at a networking event is to capture the attention of potential customers or partners, make a memorable impression, and initiate a conversation that can lead to a business opportunity or relationship. Here are some tips on how to write an effective elevator speech:

Start with a hook

Your elevator speech should start with a hook that captures the attention of your listener. This could be a question, a startling statistic, or a bold statement that addresses a common problem or pain point.

Introduce yourself and your business

After the hook, introduce yourself and your business in a clear and concise manner. Include your name, your business name, and what your business does. Keep it simple and easy to understand.

Describe your unique value proposition

Your unique value proposition is what sets you apart from your competitors. It's the benefit or solution that you offer to your target audience. Describe it in a clear and compelling way that resonates with your listener.

Provide examples or social proof

To reinforce your unique value proposition, provide examples or social proof that demonstrate how you've helped others solve their problems or achieve their goals. This could be a case study, a testimonial, or a statistic that highlights your success.

End with a call to action

Finally, end your elevator speech with a call to action that invites the listener to take the next step. This could be to schedule a meeting, visit your website, or follow you on social media. Make it easy for them to take action and continue the conversation.

It is good to remember, an elevator speech is an essential tool for networking events. It's a brief, persuasive speech that captures the attention of potential customers or partners, makes a memorable impression, and initiates a conversation that can lead to a business opportunity or relationship. By following these tips, you can write an effective elevator speech that communicates your unique value proposition and inspires action.

QUESTIONS FOR CONSIDERATION:

How can I make a good impression at the first meeting of a group?

How can I attract the right customer at an event?

What is the purpose of an elevator speech, what should it include?

In a room filled with entrepreneurs, how can I be positively remembered?

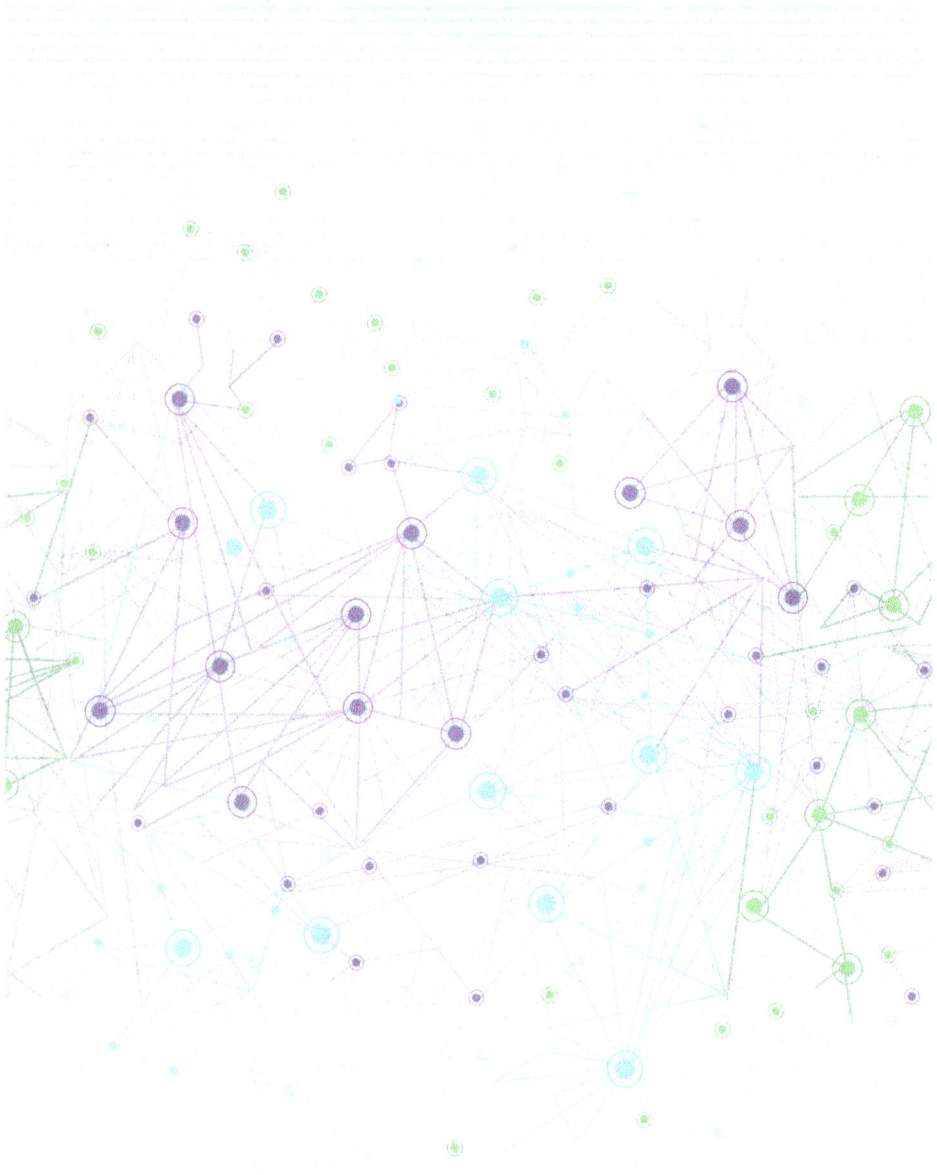

Author

Bios

DR. ANGELINE BENJAMIN (h.c.)

Dr. Angeline Benjamin is a Motivational Speaker, Action Coach with Results. She is an expert in goal setting, achievement, negotiation, and crisis management. Angeline believes in making a difference in people's lives through mentoring, coaching, and motivating others, and her audience.

Angeline started her career as a food microbiologist for Hunt Wesson Foods. She then worked for 3 other large companies. Her last large company was Taco Bell Corporation for 18 years. At Taco Bell, she discovered her passion as a coach and trainer for franchisees and restaurant management. In the last 5 years with them, she was a Food Safety Officer covering the United States. When she retired from the corporate world, Angeline started her consulting company focusing on Food Safety and Quality, coached and mentored her clients in achieving their plans and goals.

Angeline wrote her first book, "LIFE LESSONS LEADING TO SUCCESS." She is also a contributing author in Robbie Motter's book, "It's All About SHOWING UP, and the POWER is in the ASKING" and in Angela Covany's Anthology on harnessing the power of self-love and embracing the peace found in forgiveness, titled: "Love Your Haters."

She has received numerous awards for her work in business and for serving her community. In 2022, Angeline was awarded an honorary Doctorate Degree for humanitarianism and received the "SIMA Global Wall

Street Robbie Motter Award 2022" and "Global Award for Influential Women – Reaching Beyond Boundaries" and "World Super Hero" from Ladies of All Nations International (LOANI Global). She currently serves as a Global Society for Female Entrepreneurs board member and Director of the Virtual Thursday Network.

Dr. Angeline Benjamin is available for a public speaking engagement, as well as one on one or group coaching.

Email: albenjamin.bb27@gmail.com

Website: https://AngelineBenjamin.com

LinkedIn: www.linkedin.com/in/angelinebenjamin/

Facebook: www.facebook.com/angeline.benjamin.1

DR. ANGELE CADE (h.c.)

AnGèle M. Cade is a consulting expert, who has dedicated the last twenty years to helping entrepreneurs develop effective corporate structures and is recognized as the "Go To" expert for structural professional business needs.

When AnGèle is not consulting, she can be found speaking, teaching, and training on the best practices to set goals, create priorities and attain support for their vision. She is passionate about sharing down to earth, real world business experience to help solve problems and empower those around her.

Through her business ethics, personal integrity, and professional insight, and extensive experience, AnGèle truly exemplifies it's who you serve that truly makes an impact. AnGèle is the CEO and Founder of Executive on the Go, Inc. a thriving consulting firm for today's entrepreneurs.

Phone: (818) 886-4895

Email: acade@execonthego.com

Personal Website: www.angelecade.com

Business Website: www.execonthego.com

Philanthropic Website: www.akidlikeaundon.org

VIRGINIA CLARKE

Virginia was born and raised in Alberta, Canada. Her younger years, growing up on a farm, taught her many lessons about life. Lessons she carries with her to this day. Virginia lives on a small acreage with her husband, their teenage son, numerous cats, and two dogs. She lives by the motto "release your bonds and be bold!"

She is part of an organization with a series of educational workshops that have been specifically designed to support us with our healing, learning, personal and professional development.

Virginia passionate about supporting parents, persons with their wellness goals and those dealing with addictions, find their self worth.

As a Community Disability Services Worker, she provides persons with disabilities supervision, care and skill development opportunities pursue and fulfill their goals.

Virginia has over 20 years in the health/human services field, she has accumulated numerous certifications, in all positions she has worked in throughout her lifetime.

Phone: 403-506-3309

Email: unbound.bravery@gmail.com

Box 91, Site 5, RR4, Lacombe Alberta, Canada T4L2N4

DR. LAURIE DAVIS (h.c.)

Dr. Laurie Davis started her first business at the age of 12 to help support her family.

She took time out to receive her education and worked for 15 years in the public

school system and then resigned to pursue her entrepreneurial goals and has never

looked back. That was 38 years ago.

She founded and is the CEO of Self Worth the Missing Link, a series of over 600 workshops that Laurie has authored to support others with their healing, learning, personal and professional development. Laurie has worked internationally with her products expanding across all cultures. She serves adults, youth and young children in the repair and restoration of their self-worth.

Laurie has worked virtually since 2002 and has well over 25000 hours delivering her workshops on line. She has also been in broadcasting since 1998 and presently hosts her own TV show with e360 TV five days a week.

Her last book was a #1 International best-selling compilation book Ignite the Entrepreneur where she was invited to submit a chapter alongside 34 other international entrepreneurs. The book in its first day reached international status in eight categories.

Laurie is also the Director of the very first Canadian Network of GSFE.

Over the years Laurie has accumulated a multitude of awards for her work in the world.

Dr Laurie H Davis

Mentor, Entrepreneur, Educator, Certified Empowerment

Facilitator, Author

thelauriedavisshow@gmail.com

780 566 2340

Alberta, Canada

SHERRILL FRANKLIN

Sherill Franklin likes to say that she was downsized, without warning, from her homeschooling-mom job, when her children decided to grow up and leave the nest without asking permission.

As a result of this dastardly move, she was forced to find an occupation elsewhere. She has devoted her life to the service of the church and has worked to serve her community as a board member and subject matter expert for a networking group and as a member of the Conference Planning Committee of a professional society.

Sherill has received awards from prestigious organizations like the Global Society of Female Entrepreneurs, as well as commendations from members of Congress and local civic leaders.

She has been a Network Marketer for more than 10 years, and much of what she has to say has been learned in the trenches.

She and her late husband Chet raised their children in the Inland Empire. Among the values they tried to instill were the desire to be of service to others, to listen, and to invest themselves in the lives of others.

These are the same values that she finds essential in Selective Networking.

daybreak082012@gmail.com

sherillfranklin.arbonne.com

DR. MIKKI ST. GERMAIN (h.c.)

Mikki St. Germain, CEO/Founder KeepOnSharing - First Ethical Social Media Network. A published author, public speaker, and Podcast host. Mikki has worked extensively with charities and influencers. She majored in Marketing and advertising at Florida Atlantic University, which led her to the head of marketing with GTE Mobile Net (Now Verizon).

After moving to California, she became involved in United Studios of Self Defense. She received her black belt and taught women's self-defense. She became the Marketing Director for San Diego Region and was directly responsible for opening over 20 franchise locations in the San Diego area.

As the owner of Complete Coverage Football, she collaborated with the Saving Hearts Foundation with UCLA, offering free heart scans for student-athletes to prevent sudden cardiac arrest. She has worked extensively with Hands on San Diego and spearheaded a backpack drive with the San Diego Padres. She also started the San Clemente Children's toy drive with the family resource center that continues today.

- 2015 – President Obama's Presidential Lifetime Achievement Award for building a stronger nation through volunteer service.

- 2016 – Women of Influence Nominee

- 2022 – She Inspires Me Award

- 2023 - Woman of Achievement Rising Star Award

Coach Mikki St. Germain - www.KeepOnSharing.com -

www.coachmikkiandfriends.com

DR. VIVIAN A. HAIRE (h.c.)

Dr. Vivian Haire was born in Texarkana, Arkansas. She is a proud mother, grandmother, and great grandmother.

Dr. Vivian retired from Southern California Edison after twenty-four years of service. Presently she is an entrepreneur with Mary Kay Company. Her love and compassion of her fellowman allows her to receive the Recognition of Humanitarian Doctorate Award from GIA, which she will receive in Atlanta, Georgia in June 2023.

Dr. Vivian has served in the capacity of a board member in Susan B Komen, in the Inland Empire. She has also served in her local church, City of Refuge in Los Angeles, California.

In 2014 Dr. Vivian served as co-director of NAFE through 2020.She became a member of GSFE in 2020 until now. Dr. Vivian has received many awards and lifetime Achievement awards.

In 2014, Dr. Vivian received the President's to Service Award along with congratulations President's volunteer Service award Letter signed by The President of The United States, Barack Obama. In 2016 Vivian received A Lifetime Achievement Award of recognition from the Corporation for National and Community Service from the office of the President of the United States Honors signed by President Barack Obama. In 2017, Dr. Vivian received a Lifetime Achievement Award signed by President Barack Obama for the President's Volunteer Service Award. Dr. Vivian is a Two-times Breast Cancer Survivor (2009 and

2013), also 2019 D. Vivian served in the capacity as a board member in Susan B. Komen in the Inland Empire.

Certificate of Appreciation from Jill Scott Executive Director with Susan G. Komen in the Inland Empire In 2019, Dr. Vivian received an award from California Legislature Certificate of Recognition Assembly Eloise Gomez Reyes, Assembly member, 47th District, with California State Senate Certificate of Recognition from Connie M Leyva, Twentieth Senate District. Dr. Vivian received The President's Volunteer Service Award along with a letter of Congratulations of President's Volunteer Service Award signed by President Donald Trump. Dr. Vivian received the State of California Certificate of Recognition signed by Mike Morrell, State Senate, 23rd District, along with The Certificate of Recognition signed by Assemblywoman Melissa A. Melendez, 67th District. In 2021, Dr. Vivian received following Awards, State of California Certificate of Recognition signed by Melissa Melendez Member of the State 28th, State Senate, State of California Certificate of Recognition signed by District, Rosilicie Ochoa Bogh 23rd District, California Legislature Assembly Certificate of Recognition, signed by Assembly member Kelly Seyarto 67th District, City of Elsinore Certificate of Recognition for volunteering at GSFE Women's Conference signed by Timothy J Sheridan, City of Menifee signed by Mayor Bill Zimmerman Bob Karwin, Councilmember, Dean Deines, Councilmember, Matthew Liesemeyer, Councilmember, city of Riverside, County Board of Supervisors presented Certificate of Recognition for inspirational contributions to Greatness: Women's Conference signed by Jeff Hewitt 5th District Supervisor.

vvnmoore16@gmail.com. www.marykay.com/VHaire

cell 951-229-8343

DR. FELICIA HARRIS (h.c.)

Dr. Felicia Harris is an Independent Sales Director with Mary Kay. My Mary Kay journey started 21 years ago in San Diego while I was on a cruise ship.

As an Independent Mary Kay Sales Director, my ultimate goal is to share with all women and men about the importance of skin care. My tag line to everyone that I meet is "I've got you covered from your eyes to your thighs and from your lips to your hips."

Since starting my Mary Kay journey. I have had the privilege of gracing the Mary Kay Seminar stage in Dallas, Texas at our worldwide yearly convention.

My ultimate and overall goal is to help women and men feel great about their skin and skin care routines. Why? Because the skin is the largest organ on the body. One of the most rewarding compliments that can be given to me is when I am told," Thank you for taking the time to make me feel special."

I am married to my high school sweetheart, of 43 years, Arvelta Harris, Sr. We Have 3 amazing adult children (two daughters and our only son). We have four amazing glam daughters.

I debuted as a Sales Director during the pandemic in August 2021. During my first year as a Sales Director. I achieved the company's challenge of ("On The Move, Fabulous Fifties, Lead Strong and The Consistency Club.")

In my career, I have had the honor of servicing hundreds of customers. I believe that establishing trust and building lasting customer relationships is important. Because of some amazing relationships with my customers. I have earned fifty-three quarter stars which I was able to select 53 Cinderella gifts from Mary Kay. In 2016, 2021 and 2022 I was on Mary Kay's National Queens Court of Sales, which I was awarded three beautiful diamond rings. In 2012 and 2022, I was on Mary Kay's National Queens Court of Sharing and was awarded two diamond bumble bees. I have earned the privilege to drive two Mary Kay Career cars and my unit, and I are working toward that Pink Fluffy Cadillac. I am thankful to mentor and lead an amazing group of women and men that are a part of our Faith Steppers Unit. I am eternally grateful for you all.

I believe in the company's principles of God First, Family Second and Career Third. When these principles are in order, everything flows in the right direction.

I am also the advisory board member of Greater Works Today, Inc. Greater Works Today, Inc. is a 501c3 organization. Our mission is "Strengthening our cities one community at a time."

In 2021, I accepted the position of an advisory board member for Greater Works Today, Inc. I continue to work tirelessly and have partnered with Greater Works Today, Inc in the fundraising for Operation Blessings, We Care Project for Cancer Patients and Adopt The Elderly Program. Operation Blessings and the We Care Project for Cancer Patients Provides feel good body care products for patients undergoing chemotherapy and radiation treatments. The Adopt The Elderly Program provides gifts for seniors in assisted living facilities. I am so thankful to all that have partnered with me and grateful for new partnerships.

In October 2021, I was nominated by Lady Dr. Robbie Motter, to receive my Honorary Doctorate in Humanitarianism from Global International Alliance. I am thankful, humbled, and grateful that on June 17, 2023, I will be in Atlanta, Georgia to formally walk across stage to receive my degree.

The joy of knowing how many lives I have changed and how many more lives that I will change is amazing. I will continue the journey to serve my community and to be a difference maker.

DR. RAVEN L. HILDEN (h.c.)

Raven Hilden is the Founder/CEO of MilVet, a nonprofit dedicated to supporting deployed troops, veterans, and their families. Her dedication to servant leadership has helped create programs aimed at making a positive impact in the lives of others and was awarded an Honorary Doctorate of Humanitarianism in 2023.

Raven earned an associate in criminal justice and Bachelor of Science degree in Human Services/Management at the University of Phoenix. Her education and experience inspired her to create a nonprofit to connect active military/veterans and their families to resources in the community. MilVet – Military & Veteran Support Services, is a nonprofit that currently supports thousands of deployed troops all over the world and veterans every month, where she currently serves as the CEO.

MilVet won Nonprofit of the Year 2022 by the 67th California State Assembly and Menifee Chamber of Commerce, best nonprofit 2021 by the Murrieta/Wildomar Chamber of Commerce and was voted as Top-Rated Nonprofit in 2021 from Great Nonprofits. MilVet also received the honorary Service Above Self award at the Murrieta Field of Honor 2021 among other awards. The nonprofit has been featured in the Press Enterprise, Valley News, Arizona Central, Business Wire, San Diego Voyager, Yahoo Finance, Arizona The Mix 101.3, IHeart Radio and more.

Raven's professional experience includes work for the California State Senate and State Assembly as a District

Representative performing case management and as a community liaison for elected officials. She currently has a web design and marketing business.

Raven has earned the Presidential Lifetime Achievement Award by three seated Presidents. She attributes her success to a supportive community and network of friends and volunteers that strive to make a difference in their communities.

Her passion for helping others shows in the difference she continues to make an impact in the community as she currently serves on numerous veteran committees and is a member of the Global Society for Female Entrepreneurs (GSFE) and the Professional Women's Roundtable. She earned University of Phoenix's Leadership Impact Award in 2019 and in 2021 she received the 100 Women Global award and 100 Successful Women International. In 2022 she won the Joan Sparkman Unity Award - an incredible honor!

She is a proud member of the National Society of Leadership and Success 2022 and released a bestselling book in 2022 titled, "A Veteran's Story – Courage and Honor," a compilation of stories written by 30 local veterans.

Raven is married to a Marine Corps Veteran, and together they have 5 children and 2 grandchildren. Her passion is to help honor those who served and to help inspire others to reach new heights.

Founder/CEO Milvet
Ceo@milvet.org - www.milvet.org

KRISTIE JACOBO

My name is Kristie Jacobo. I am a Gas Pipeline Transmission Project Manager, mother, and enthusiast for biohacking activation projects to improve health and wellness. I have always been drawn to the art of organization and leadership, which led me to pursue a career in project management. I enjoy the fast-paced nature of my industry and I thrive in conflict management and the ability to make rapid decisions in critical situations. Perhaps one of the keys to my successful career history is my ability to effectively communicate with stakeholders at all levels and find relatability.

Outside of my professional life, I am a proud mother to my twelve-year-old son. There is no guide to raising a son as a widow and solo parent. Balancing the demands of a full-time career, part-time side gig, and motherhood has taught me the importance of time management, organization, and adaptability. I've also gained insight of the true meaning of empathy and overcoming obstacles.

In my free time, I find solace in my garden. Gardening allows me to connect with nature and create a peaceful sanctuary. It is a constant reminder of the beauty and resilience of life. Through gardening I have learned patience, an eye for detail, an appreciation of Mother Nature, and the ability to adapt to changing conditions. Writing is another creative outlet for me. I enjoy penning down my thoughts, experiences, and challenging myself to communicate and articulate my experience and thoughts through the power of storytelling. My hope is to inspire and motivate others.

I tell my friends and family that I find a piece of joy in every day. Throughout my journey, this comes easier some days and harder on other days. Positivity is a mindset that keeps me wanting to strive to be better for myself, my son, and everyone that I get to share my time with along the way. I look forward to the next chapter and I hope you enjoy my chapter in this collaboration.

CAROL LATHAM

Following a career as a fashion model, television actor, teacher, and image

consultant, Carol has for almost 30 years, owned a fashion show production company – Fashion Events Unlimited. Her business has been recognized for excellence in business practices by the Anaheim Chamber of Commerce, the American Business Woman's Association and Women's Referral Services Orange County and Los Angeles. As a partner with Neora - a global wellness company - she encourages people to live their best lives. In addition, she is the Community Outreach Specialist for Anaheim's Muzeo Museum and Cultural Center.

Countless hours are devoted to community service, as a volunteer, and she currently serves on the boards of a variety of non-profit organizations. These include the Anaheim Community Foundation, Altrusa International Foundation of Anaheim, Inc., Altrusa International District Eleven Boards. In 2003-05 she was the District Governor overseeing clubs in California, Arizona and in 2005-2007 and 2013-2015 served as an International Director on the Altrusa International Board.

She has received awards recognizing her community involvement in Anaheim. These include the 1998 'Woman of the Year' California State Legislature District 34; Small Business 'Woman of the Year' in 1999 by the Anaheim Chamber of Commerce; the 2002 Cypress College Americana Award - Anaheim's Citizen of the Year. In 2018 she was named the Woman of the Year for 29th

Senatorial District and a Woman of Distinction for the 46th Congressional District and in 2019 was awarded the prestigious Altrusa International Eleanor Roosevelt Humanitarian Award.

Since moving from Toronto, Canada, Carol and her husband, Lindsay have made Anaheim their home.

carollatham119@gmail.com

(714) 719-9922

DR. TYARA LEE (h.c.)

Tyara Lee aka Coach Tee Lee is a wife, mom an ordained and affirmed Pastor/Prophetess. Out of all of her titles she prefers to be called Coach Tee Lee. She holds dear to the three E's Educate, Empower & Encourage as she leads and empowers everyone she comes across.

Coach Tee Graduated from Pasadena City College with AA in Social Behavioral Sciences and her Major is Business, she has an Honorary Doctorate from Global International Alliance University in Humanitarianism for all of the work she has done changing and reaching and changing the lives of millions. She is the CEO and founder of She Is Foundation Network, Inc. 501(c)(3) Nonprofit Organization that supplies resources for women globally which was featured on national tv and local radio stations. Coach Tee Lee is the CEO and founder of My Marketing Needs, LLC providing business with all of their printing, marketing, hiring, and coaching needs.

Coach Tee loves to play and coach basketball, play the drums, dance, and create Empowering Events such as vision board classes, resource fairs, entrepreneur networking events and more. She competes in beauty pageants to spread awareness about her platform "SHE IS" for her nonprofit. Coach Tee Lee had won many pageants, but most recently was crowned the first United States America's Mrs. California 2020. Mrs. California Prime 2022, and Mrs. USA Prime 2023 first runner up.

Email-MyMarketingNeedsLLC@gmailcom
Phone: 802-618-0038

DR. JEANNETTE LEHOULLIER (h.c.)

Dr. H.C. Jeannette LeHoullier enjoys sharing JOY through singing, writing & giving. She is known as "Joyful Diva" by many of her business acquaintances, for her unique laugh and bringing "sunshine" into other's lives, as some say.

She grew up in Bakersfield, California singing Acapella gospel hymns in church, regularly singing harmony with the congregation's 4-part harmony songs. Her family moved to Alaska where she started high school, married, and started a family.

Jeannette has been regaining her operatic voice after a vocal injury that led her to hide her voice for over 40 years. Local Karaoke in Menifee, CA has given her a boost to begin singing and performing again, along with the numerous support of her GSFE (Global Society of Female Entrepreneurs) which are her special global sisters.

While in Alaska, she was selected to sing the female lead (Mother) by the Italian Composer Gian Carlo Menotti for the seasonal Christmas Opera "Amahl and the Night Visitors," she was age 17 at the time (Senior year of high school).

Recently, she has performed for the International Hollywood Talent Show in Hollywood and Nutcracker – The Musical at the Temecula Old Town Theater.

Her business is JEANNETTE'S JOY – aiding Women and Seniors needing TLC business assistance in adapting to their often unknown and frustrating newer technology devices, laptops, apps. She also provided a customized liaison service to assist with challenging for administrative support with her highly valued "listening ear." She is a wonderful friend known for practicing the "Golden Rule" of treating others the way they want and prefer to be treated.

Jeannette volunteered for 2 years at the Kay Cisneros Senior Center for the City of Menifee, before starting her Senior Tech Tutor business (DJ's Virtual Management/ Senior Tech Tutor.

Jeannette is a diversified "Servant Leadership" expert with a Bachelor of Science degree (2003) in Organizational Leadership from BIOLA University (Bible Institute of Los Angeles University).

In 2023, she graciously accepted the prestigious Honorary Doctorate Degree of Humanitarianism from the Global International Alliance University (GIA) – in Humanitarianism honoring her over 50 years as a humanitarian.

Jeannette has over 40 years of administrative experience: as a Leader, Manager, Network Administrator, COBOL Business Programmer (Business Language), Website Creator, Tech Customer Support Manager, Network Administrator, Website Manager, and Liaison Guru. She has managed websites for herself and for Business. Jeannette has created and managed self-created Websites and Social Media sites. She has also provided Administrative Employee Support to both Paid and Volunteer staff.

Jeannette is also a skilled Professional Leader as the former Chief Executive Officer (CEO) for The HealthCare Foundation Orange County (HFOC), a 501c3 health grant giving Foundation – which originated from the first hospital in Orange County, CA – Western Medical Center Hospitals.

Her business JEANNETTE'S JOY became more accurate in representing the "many hats" she has worn for years. It is the result of rebranding her businesses JEANNETTE'S JOY and DJ's Virtual Management/Senior Tech Tutor and honoring her overall brand of "JOYFUL DIVA" and "GOLDEN RULE" advocate (treating others how I would want to be treated – but with a twist – treating others the way they want to be treated)! Joyful Diva Jeannette is a great friend with compassion in masse. She is a cheerful. Joyful Diva has an infectious laugh (with a ringtone for purchase!).

Joyful Diva rebranded her business in 2021 in order to serve her community and target audiences with extended value from her lifetime of service, degrees, and experience – both in the small businesses sector and her focused target audience of women and Senior Citizens.

JEANNETTE'S JOY serves both personal clients and smaller Entrepreneur business. Jeannette is the former Chief Executive Officer (CEO) of The HealthCare Foundation for Orange County (CA). HFOC awards grants to non-profits with children and women health programs in the central Orange County, CA area.

Jeannette has been honored recently with an Honorary

Doctorate degree in Humanitarianism.

She is also humbled and excited to be recording songs with Marneen Lynne Fields of Heavenly Waterfall Songs and Productions for her creative and heartfelt original upcoming movie "Who's Gonna Take Care of Me?."

DR. SARA M. LYPPS (h.c.), MBA

I am extremely passionate about educating, empowering, & encouraging woman and their families to get their finances in order. I am a Comprehensive Financial Advisor offering a wide variety of services to meet all of your retirement planning needs. I take a 360° approach to looking at your current plan and determining where there may be gaps that need filling in or areas that require attention or improvement. There is no such thing as a "one size fits all" method when it comes to your financial future; every client gets a custom financial plan as well as a customized course of action. There are many cares and concerns that we will address, leaving you with a better overall understanding of where you are now and where to go from here, which offers you a greater peace of mind.

My ultimate goal is to provide my clients with freedom from doubt, worries, and anxieties around all of their finances and their financial future.

WHY ME?? Because I've been there. I lost my husband tragically at a very young age and wasn't prepared. I'm a mom raising four children on my own and I get it. There are a lot of financial advisors giving you advice that sounds good to them, but many are simply looking out for their own skin. I am proud to say that being a Fiduciary for my clients allows me to serve them with utmost integrity and I always put the needs of my clients first. I little more about me: I also have an extensive real estate and construction background which gives me a very unique edge over my competition. I'm a numbers girl who knows how to get the job done, is passionate about people, leads from the heart, and always goes the extra mile to do the right thing for my clients.

WHAT'S NEXT? I'm creating three programs for financial literacy for young people. The first is for adolescence, the second is for teenagers, and finally a program for young adults. I believe it's important to learn the skills to pay the bills and save from a young age, and our school system simply hasn't caught up yet to suit their educational needs. I'm also working on two books myself, one that's a quick guide to your finances and the other that dives deep into my personal story, triumph from tragedy. Recently, I was nominated by Lady Dr. Robbie Motter to receive an Honorary Doctorate this month which will be taking place in Atlanta, GA. Stay tuned, I'm really going places!

DR. SUSIE MIERZWIK (h.c.)

Susie Mierzwik is a retired teacher who received the Teacher of the Year award in 2000 from her district in southern California. She does volunteer work with various charities, including Samaritan's Purse which sends gift boxes of essential items to children in third world countries. Senator Mike Morrel presented her with a community service award in 2014.

Since retiring from education in 2012, she has devoted herself to building a health and wellness business. It is a cutting-edge technology from LifeWave that uses phototherapy and stem cell regeneration to assist the body in healing and eliminating pain. Since 2009 she has been building her business, and now has clients around the globe.

In 2020 she was a contributing author to an anthology called "2020, A Year of Faith with the Information Diva. She also has chapters in two other books coming out in 2022: " The Impact of One Voice" and "Love Your Haters". Her Memoir titled, "Sow in Tears, Reap in Joy" were published in the summer of 2022.

She and her husband Steve live in southern California where they share six children and five grandchildren. They enjoy travelling in Europe, Hawaii, and have taken two safaris to Tanzania, Africa. Susie and Steve stay active with biking, hiking, and square dancing with local groups.

Website: https://susiemierzwik.com Email: kinderkat9@gmail.com

Email: kinderkat9@gmail.com - Phone: 909-709-3075

DR. RAMIN MODIRI (h.c.)

Ramin Modiri, Entrepreneur, Educator, Licensed International Financial Analyst, MBA MS Degrees in Finance Certified Financial Planner, Chartered Financial Consultant, BS Actuarial Science and Mathematics, Certified Fund Specialist

Ramin has an extensive background in the financial world. Prior to his retirement he was a portfolio and investment manager for 33 years. His love of the sport of soccer and with many years of coaching under his belt, he combined that with his financial expertise, to manage investment portfolios for Soccer professional.

However, his passion these days is education. For the past 15 years Ramin has mentored over 1000 undergraduates and graduates who learn from him on a weekly basis. These accomplished individuals being mentored by him come from a wide source of universities throughout America. Berkeley, UCLA, MIT, USC just to name a few.

Ramin takes great pleasure in educating others now so the average person can grasp the importance of building fortunes and legacies, and just how to do that particularly for our next generation.

Website: https://rmsmartinvesting.com

LADY AMBASSADOR DR. ROBBIE MOTTER (h.c)

Robbie Motter is the founder of GSFE (Global Society for Female Entrepreneurs) and for over 29 years served as the Global Coordinator for NAFE (National Association of Female Executives), she left that volunteer position in April 2020 to devote more time to her nonprofit work with GSFE.

The non-profit which she founded in 2017 is a 501 c3 non-profit and does an annual GSFE woman's conference," Lady in Blue Sapphire awards", "Kindness Day" and many other events.

GSFE does mentoring, training, coaching women as well as doing collaborations with other organizations. Many of the collaborations are with groups that she can nominate her members for awards to help them build their brand. Their mission is to empower, inspire, mentor, educate and connect women so they become successful entrepreneurs.

She is also the author of volume 1 and 2 which became a #1 US and #1 International Best-Selling book called "It's All About Showing Up and the Power is in the Asking," she also wrote her third book "How to Rise Up and A.C.H.I.E.V.E A woman's leader manual for life and is a co author of numerous #1 best sellers.

Over the years Robbie has received over 180 awards for her work with women. The variety of awards can be seen on her website robbiemotter.com

Robbie spent 25 years in Corporate America before

becoming and Entrepreneur. She founded and currently runs a successful nonprofit. She is a Marketing/PR Consultant, radio show host, event planner, a #1 US and International Best Selling Author. She is a certified public speaker. In May of 2022 in Atlanta, Geogia she received an Honorary Humanitarian Doctor's Degree for her work over the years and in December 2022 was presented her Lady title in London England

To learn more about Robbie you can visit gsfeus.com and robbiemotter.com. She can also be found on Facebook and Linkedin as Robbie Motter , her email is rmotter@aol.com and she can be reached on WhatsApp by phone 951-255-9200 (her cell phone number).

CHRISTINE PARK

Christine Park is a mother, grandmother, and retired businesswoman originally from Northwestern Pennsylvania. She graduated from Penn State Cosmetology and attended Penn State University and The Art Institute of Pittsburgh.

As a businesswoman, she had several businesses with multiple locations throughout Ohio. Christine holds a Cosmetology license in Pennsylvania, teaching licenses in Ohio, Security Licenses in multiple states and is an ordained minister with an honorary doctorate in Divinity. Christine was honored as 2014-2015

Inductee into National Association of Professional Women's VIP WOMAN OF THE YEAR CIRCLE for excellence, leadership, and commitment to her profession, while encouraging the achievement of Professional Women. Christine is an active member of Global Society of Female Entrepreneurs and is the head of production organization for Heavenly Waterfall Productions' upcoming film, "Who's Gonna Take Care of Me?" In her spare time, you can find Christine singing at karaoke as well as at a few local events. "Life is full of challenges, conquer each one as you journey through the seasons of life."

DR. CHERIE REYNOLDS (h.c.)

Cherie Reynolds is an Entrepreneur with great expertise in marketing and connecting individuals and also is a #1 award winning US and International Author.

Currently CEO of Cheri's Energy Solutions 2023 where she is leading the international expansion of the fastest growing renewable energy company in the world.

She had a long career in Sales and Marketing working with numerous firms and organizations like Chambers of Commerce's and corporations she also owed an Executive Housekeeping and Janitorial Service,

She is currently serving as the codirector of the Oceanside Global Society of Female Entrepreneurs. GSFE a 501 c3 nonprofit, and over the years has served as an Ambassador of the Riverside, Hemet, and San Jacinto Chamber of Commerce's

She attended High School in Bitburg, Germany, the University of Maryland and received an AA Psychology in Munich Germany and also attended Fullerton Jr College in Fullerton, CA

On June 15, 2023, she will receive an Honorary Humanitarian Doctorate degree in Atlanta, Ga., for her work in serving her communities over the years. She is a single mom of two daughters, has five grandchildren and one great grandchild.

She was born in Ca and currently resides in North County,

CA., she can be reached at cherischallenge@gmail.com, 909-238-5790.

ARVEE ROBINSON

Arvee Robinson, The Master Speaker Trainer, international keynote speaker, and three-time bestselling author, captivates her audiences with high-energy, high-content, interactive presentations filled with vivid stories. Her audiences have fun while learning workable strategies they can put into action immediately. Arvee has presented more than forty-five hundred motivational keynotes and content-rich educational programs all over the world. She has shared the stage with speaking giants Mark Victor Hansen, Brian Tracy, Les Brown, Sharon Lechter, Loral Langemeier, Tom Hopkins, and many others.

As an in-demand speaking coach for two decades, Arvee has taught more than five thousand business owners how to attract more clients, generate unlimited leads, and grow their businesses fast by clearly communicating what they do. She teaches simple, proven systems for delivering persuasive presentations, magnetic introductions, five-minute business showcases, and compelling promotional videos. Arvee has helped hundreds of individuals eliminate nervousness, command their audiences' attention, and deliver sales-winning speeches.

Arvee is a published author of *Speak Up Get Clients: How to Use Public Speaking as a Marketing Strategy to Attract High-Paying Clients*. She has published chapters in six collaborative books, number-one bestseller *The Impact of One Voice*, Volume I, and Volume II, number-one bestseller *Jumpstart Your _____* Volume VI, number-one bestseller *Live the Life You Love*, number-one bestseller *Ready Aim*

Captivate, Inspiration to Realization, and *Profitable Social Media.* She is also the host of the *Million Dollar Speaker Podcast.*

On a personal note, Arvee holds a BS degree in Information Systems, has achieved many outstanding awards and trophies, and lives in Southern California.

DR. AVIC RONQUILLO-DE CASTRO (h.c.)

Avic Ronquillo-De Castro is a successful entrepreneur, administrator, and accounting specialist with a passion for managing, coordinating, and accounting. Born on July 16, 1960, in Manila, Philippines, parents are Col. Cenon & Adoracion Ronquillo, family are Dennis De Castro, Darwin & Marden, Lucky, my service pet dog, a US citizen/PhilDual, residing in Winchester, CA, USA.

Avic's professional journey began with her love for accounting, which led her to become a QuickBooks PRO Accounting Specialist. With her sharp mind and attention to detail, she quickly became an expert in her field and began providing valuable accounting services to small and medium-sized businesses.

Over time, Avic's expertise expanded to include management, coordination, and she became an event coordinator, helping businesses plan and execute successful events. Avic's strong organizational skills and attention to detail ensured that every event was a success.

 Avic is also an international social media digital marketing partner. She has helped many businesses establish their online presence and reach their target audience through social media marketing.

Avic's dedication to her work have made her a respected figure in the business community. She continues to innovate and grow her business, always striving to provide the best possible service to her clients.

Today, Avic is an accomplished entrepreneur with a thriving business. Her experience in management, coordination, accounting, event planning, and social digital marketing make her a valuable asset to any business looking to grow and succeed.

DR. KAYE SHEFFIELD (h.c.), M.S., CCC-SLP

I currently live in Calimesa, California. I grew up as an Air Force brat, living in 18 different locations and attending 15 different schools including 3 different colleges and universities. Having attended and graduated from high school in Germany, we were able to enjoy many different experiences, languages, and learned about different cultures. I attended San Jose State University in California and took all the course work and exams to obtain a Master of Arts degree, only to find out that they required a thesis besides taking the exams to graduate. As a newlywed living in Southern California, I found it difficult, if not impossible to finish the thesis. I went back to college after 20 years, to Loma Linda University, as a single parent, after my 3 children were established in school. I could then work a part-time job and attend and finish my Master of Science degree in Speech and Language Pathology and attend activities with my children and church.

Work sites after my degree included hospitals, convalescent homes, private therapy, universities, and mainly working in the schools. I retired after 22 years working in the school districts but have not stopped working as a Speech Therapist/Speech-Language Pathologist.

Currently I am an affiliate with a worldwide Health and Wellness company and Dr. Sears a Certified Health Coach.

I have 3 wonderful successful children, 4 fantastic grandchildren and 2 super bonus children.

I love to dance, travel, learn, and help others through

church, GSFE, Speech and Language Pathology, and my dance clubs. Having just finished writing a second for me, section of a book compilation, it is an answer to prayer and one of my self-goals. I am delighted to share my thoughts and experiences and I hope that you enjoy reading this section.

Email: kaye_slp@msn.com

† DR. DEBORAH THORNE (h.c.)

The Information Diva, Dr. Deborah Thorne (h.c.), was an award-winning, internationally known author, coach, trainer, speaker, and host of **The Leverage Conference for Speakers, Authors, and Entrepreneurs.** She advised and supported women entrepreneurs, she encouraged them to do business like a woman, not like a man... She E.O. ...not C.E.O.

The Information Diva was a connector and opportunity creator. She advised and supported women (and some men) to transition from employee to six-figure entrepreneurs. Starting where they were, she helped to reduce their learning curve and save time through demystifying business principles and systems, creating income-generating businesses, not glorified hobbies.

ANGEL TOUSSAINT

I was born and raised in Anchorage, Alaska. I lived in Alaska from birth to 37 years of age. Growing up we never traveled to any other part of the country. All vacations were to other cities in Alaska. One day at age 37 I found the courage to leave Alaska and try living in another part of the country. I chose Northern California.

I have had more vocations than most. The longest stint was in the corporate arena. In addition to my W2 positions I always had some form of entrepreneurial venture on the side. I remember when a friend said, "Angel, you are a serial entrepreneur," we laughed and I replied, "true and until I find the entrepreneurial venture that is right for me I will continue to be a serial entrepreneur." My first entrepreneur venture was selling Tupperware when I was working as a bank teller in my late teens early 20's. I have always held a career/job to pay my bills and keep a roof over my head, but I never gave up on my entrepreneurial dream.

I am happy I never gave up on my entrepreneurial dream. Today I have my own company in the health and wellness industry. I love getting new customers who are willing to make a few simple changes in their life to improve their health. Their health improvement brings me the greatest joy.

I look forward to being of service to you. Call or text me at   951-499-4759. Visit my website at https://theserioushealthpeople.com

AMB. DR. JOAN E. WAKELAND (h.c.)

Dr. Joan E Wakeland is an Author, International Speaker, and an Empowerment Facilitator.

Presently, she is the Director of the Riverside affiliate of the Global Society of Female Entrepreneurs in California.

Over the years, she has received many Awards including the "The Lifetime Achievement Award" from the last three Presidents of the United States. She also received the "Call to Service" and numerous awards from Senators, Congress & dignitaries.

She won the title for Ms. Elegance International in the Woman of Achievement Pageant in September 2021. In December 2021, she was honored as Citizen of the Month by The Mayor and City Delegates for her service to the city of Menifee.

Joan recently received the "She Inspires Me Award" (SIMA) International Global Award from London, England.

In 2022 she was awarded an honorary humanitarian doctorate degree for her service to others.

In 2024 Joan was awarded the Miracle Women Award from LOANI in London, England

If you are interested in being an affiliate for a Global Company visit https://livegoodtour.com/healthyhelpers

Contact

Email: joanewakeland@gmail.com

Facebook: https://facebook.com/thehealthyhelpers

951-400-5341

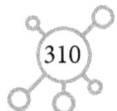

DR. DOROTHY WOLONS (h.c.)

Dorothy Wolons is a dynamic individual who was born and raised in Detroit, Michigan. Currently residing in Menifee, California, Dorothy has embraced her surroundings and has become an integral part of the community.

Dorothy's professional journey began in the field of finance, where she spent the early years of her career as a Collections Manager, after graduating from Wayne State University. Her passion for helping others led her to inspire and educate certified students in the collection field. However, seeking new challenges, she eventually transitioned to running a national sales team before venturing into entrepreneurship. Dorothy successfully owned and operated two of her own retail stores, showcasing her exceptional business acumen.

Further exploring her potential, Dorothy found her calling at the Menifee Valley Chamber of Commerce, where she served as the CEO and Director for an impressive tenure of 10 years. During her time in this esteemed position, she accomplished remarkable feats and garnered invaluable experience in the chamber industry. Dorothy's dedication and commitment to the community she served were truly commendable. She regularly volunteered and actively participated in numerous gratifying organizations, including being a member of the GSFE (Global Society for Female Executives).

Dorothy's personal life is also filled with happiness and fulfillment. As a devoted mother and loving grandmother, family holds a special place in her heart. She cherishes her time spent with her children, grandchildren, and her partner Rafael. In addition to her family commitments, Dorothy has also achieved recognition as an international best-selling author, demonstrating her exceptional writing skills.

Beyond her professional and personal accomplishments, Dorothy also carries the title of an ordained minister. Her faith and spirituality have guided her throughout her life, providing her with a strong moral compass and a genuine desire to help others.

With a wealth of experience, commendable achievements, and a heart full of compassion, Dorothy continues to make a positive impact on the world around her.

Amb. Dr. Joan Wakeland (h.c)

The Power of Networking

I feel so honored to work with a team of dedicated professionals who spent many hours to make "The Power of Networking" a reality. The idea was conceived by Amb. Dr. Joan Wakeland in a work shop on "Self-worth, the missing link" facilitated by Dr. Laurie Davis . This book is designed to be a workbook for workshops, webinars, or Seminars. It is ideal for students and beginners.

"The Power of Networking" also serves as a reminder for those who have been networking for years! It addresses so many aspects of networking.

The Chapters were written by best-selling authors, global influencers, social media experts, business professionals, and some individuals who were doing their first book!

Networking can help you to change your net worth!

Global Society of Female Entrepreneurs (GSFE) is a nonprofit organization dedicated to empowering and educating women. The CEO and founder Ambassador Lady Dr. (h.c.) Robbie Motter has dedicated her life to empowering women. I met Robbie in 2001 when I started living in the Menifee Valley.

She became one of my Mentors and introduced me to Serving in the community. I was able to build relationships with many individuals that I would never have met without the support from this lady. She even introduced me to my fiancé!

I have had the privilege of living in the United States, and I am grateful to the many people who have supported me in my journey!

If you are interested in networking with a great group of individuals who are passionate and interested in helping others you can join the GSFE networking group by visiting gsfe.us

I love to connect individuals and I have met some amazing people.

If you are interested in building relationships internationally you may want to contact Prof. Dr Caroline Makaka from the LOANI organization. Her information is at the end of the foreword.

If you are interested in Reclaiming Your Self-worth and becoming an Empowerment Facilitator you can contact Dr. h.c. Laurie Davis from Canada. I received a wealth of knowledge from her. You can find her contact information in her bio on page 168.

We deliver a series of educational workshops that have been specifically designed to support us with our healing, our learning, and our personal and professional development.

Our lineup of over 1000 workshops include products programs and services for adults, youth, and young children.

We have been working virtually since 2002 and provide a safe space with no more than six clients in a workshop.

We are the how-to people. Whatever situation you find yourself in we undoubtedly have worked with others in a similar place.

To learn more about us please visit The Dr. Laurie Davis Show at www.e360tv.com. Email Dr Laurie at thelauriedavisshow@gmail.com or text 780 909 8571.

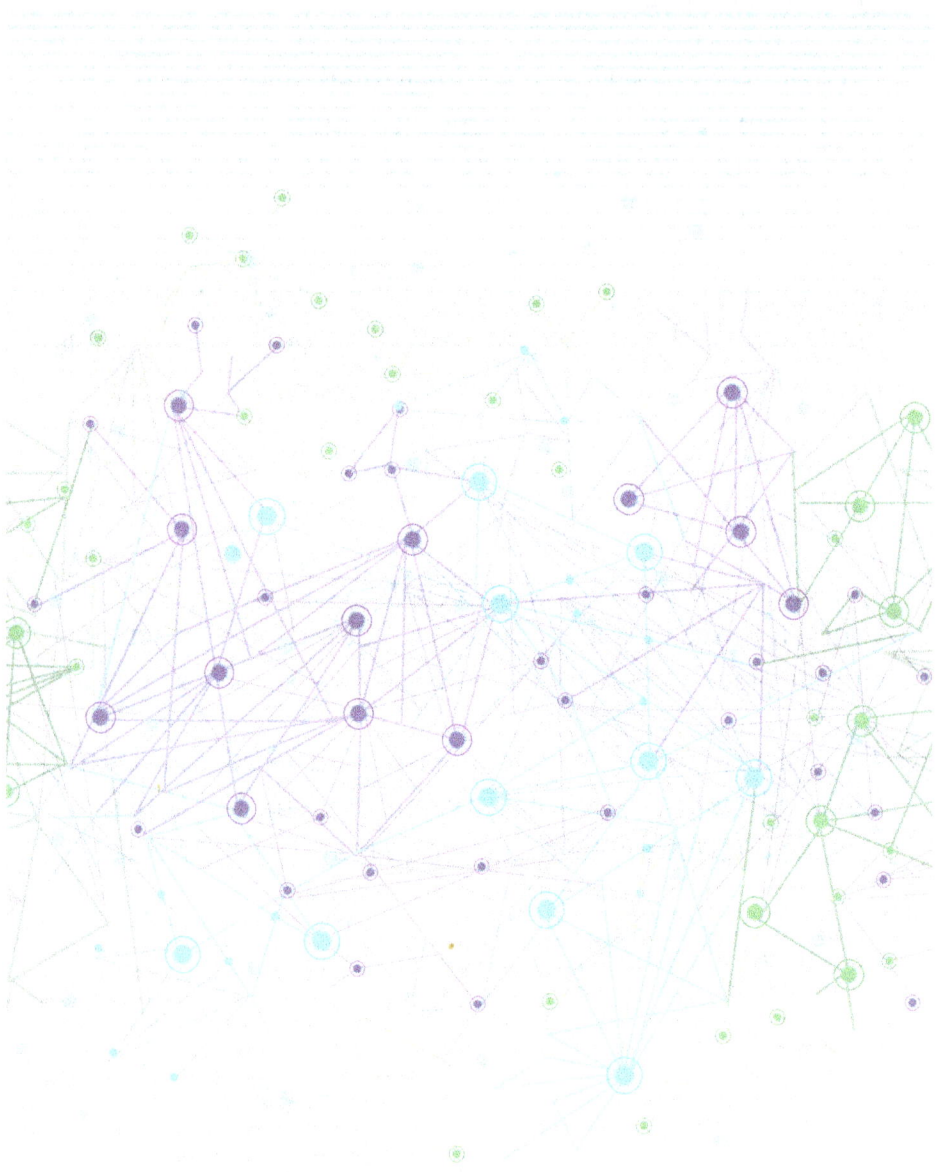

TRIBUITE TO DR. DEBORAH THORNE (h.c.)

"Kindness Day" is being celebrated in November. GSFE has lost one of our dear beloved sisters, Dr. Deborah Thorne (h.c.). We are grieving her, and all around us we are constantly reminded that this journey we are on together is not forever; we are not promised tomorrow. So, do not let one day in November be your legacy and limit for kindness. You have every day for 12 months to sharpen your kindness skills every year. Be the one who reaches out to other members. Be the one who asks what do you need. Be the one who donates whatever you're not wearing in your closet. Be the inspiration for someone facing a challenge.

Deborah was kind. She mailed out little gifts at no cost just because. She prayed for others. She spoke her mind with no take backs. But you can be assured that her advice was to guide you to a better place in life, not just to hear the sound of her own voice. And now Deborah is not here with us anymore.

Let her Legacy be the reminder to be kind and considerate members of the Global Society For Female Entrepreneurs every day. Deborah, you will be missed. Go with God! And be healed of all your burdens and pains from now until the end of time.

Amen!"

Katherine Orho, Director GSFE Tech Chapter wrote the kind words above.

Dr. Deborah Thorne (h.c.), our GSFE sister, had a big heart for others. She honored each one by sending a personal greeting card by mail, to brighten our day. She never forgot a Birthday. Deborah showed us how to do business as a She.E.O and not a C.E.O. She showed us how to do business like a woman not a man. Dr. Deborah was a connector, supporter, and a sister in Faith. REST in PEACE dear Deborah. Your Race is Won.

When I called Dr. Deborah and asked her to write the chapter on "Following up" she said she would. She expressed how busy she was but committed to sending me her chapter. She kept her word! That's how she did business! She promised, She delivered! She did not keep her knowledge to herself. She did not take her knowledge to the grave! She passed the baton to the next generation! What a beautiful Legacy, a life well lived!

Dr. Deborah was a sister and a friend, it is an honor to dedicate this book to her posthumously.

Amb. Dr. Joan E Wakeland (h.c)

Humanitarianism